From Crisis to Comeback

Overcome Business Failure and Thrive Again

RANDY EACHUS

DEDICATION

Chloe, your creativity and natural ability to lead others is truly inspiring.

Austin, your strength and competitive mindset pushes me to overcome any challenge.

Wendy, you are my foundation and love. None of this is possible without you.

CONTENTS

ACKNOWLEDGMENTS

This book is dedicated to everyone who has ever experienced the sting of failure in business, only to discover that it is not an end but a beginning. It's a testament to the unyielding support of colleagues, friends, and family, who remain a beacon of light in both our successes and trials, teaching us the power of forgiveness and steadfast belief in our abilities. It is in their unwavering presence that we find the courage to treat each misstep as a lesson, to view each failure not as defeat, but a testament to our strength and potential. As we venture through this journey of growth and reinvention, I extend my heartfelt gratitude to these companions for their pivotal role in transforming our trials into triumphs.

CHAPTER 1

FACING REALITY
CONFRONTING THE TRUTH

Acknowledging the Situation

In the vast and unforgiving landscape of the business world, moments arise that test the mettle of even the most seasoned entrepreneurs. These are the moments that can define a leader's legacy, the pivotal crossroads where decisions must be made with unwavering courage and steely determination. This chapter delves into the profound significance of acknowledging the situation, a critical step towards charting a course to redemption when faced with a faltering enterprise.

Once upon a time, the business thrived, an emblem of success and a beacon of innovation. Yet, in the cyclical nature of commerce, challenges can rear their heads with unrelenting vigor. Market dynamics shift, competitors emerge, and unforeseen circumstances can conspire to rock the foundations of even the mightiest of ventures.

For a leader, coming to terms with such adversities can be an uphill battle. The temptation to retreat into a realm of denial can be alluring, for acknowledging the situation mandates a confrontation with realities that may evoke discomfort and uncertainty. The allure of hope, that things will spontaneously mend, can veil the stark truths lurking beneath the surface.

However, true leaders are not beguiled by illusions of temporary respite. They possess the audacity to confront the storm head-on, to gaze unflinchingly into the tempest of challenges before them. The act of acknowledging the situation is not an act of defeat; rather, it is a testament to the indomitable spirit of a leader who refuses to be cowed by the odds.

In the boardrooms and corner offices, whispered conversations may attempt to shroud the bitter realities in euphemisms and half-truths. But authenticity, transparency, and candidness become the hallmarks of genuine leadership. In this moment of reckoning, the truest measure of a leader's integrity is revealed. Employees, investors, and stakeholders alike seek honesty, and it is in the vulnerable acknowledgment of a situation's gravity that trust finds fertile ground to blossom.

The consequences of evading reality can be dire, ripples of repercussions that echo through the company's core. A crisis deferred is not a crisis averted, for festering wounds can poison even the most prosperous ventures. By prolonging the reckoning, leaders inadvertently jeopardize the very survival of the business they hold dear.

Yet, when leaders embrace the unvarnished truth, a gateway to transformation emerges. Adversity is not a force to be evaded but a crucible in which leaders and businesses are forged anew. It is here, in this crucible, that the essence of leadership is distilled, where decisions of profound consequence are born.

Acknowledging the situation allows leaders to marshal their resources, to gather their teams around a shared understanding of the challenges that lie ahead. In unity, a collective resilience can emerge, fostering the birth of innovative solutions and the fortitude to endure the hardships that may ensue.

The journey of acknowledgment is not devoid of discomfort; on the contrary, it requires unwavering self-awareness and humility. It is an acceptance that fallibility is an inherent facet of human experience, and that missteps can serve as a compass for the future. By examining past decisions with a critical eye, leaders gain insights that become guiding stars for the path forward.

In the pages of history, there are tales of leaders who navigated the treacherous seas of adversity with sagacity and grace. They did not waver when confronted with their business's frailty; instead, they girded themselves with resilience and determination. In the crucible of challenge, they forged a legacy that transcended the moment, a testament to the indomitable spirit of leadership.

Acknowledging the situation is not an act of capitulation, but a testament to leadership's strength and authenticity. It is the embrace of realities that demand confrontation, and the pursuit of transformation amidst adversity. In the annals of business lore, it is these leaders who illuminate the way for others to follow, illuminating a path to redemption and triumph against all odds.

Confronting the Truth: Admitting that Your Business is in Trouble

In the tumultuous terrain of business, leaders are often portrayed as unwavering pillars of strength, destined to guide their enterprises through all storms unscathed. Yet, in the annals of true leadership, it is the ability to confront the harshest truths that sets apart the extraordinary from the ordinary. Admitting that your business is in trouble is not a sign of weakness; rather, it is a testament to your strength as a leader – a strength that emerges from humility, self-awareness, and an unyielding commitment to face adversity head-on. The journey of entrepreneurship is strewn with both triumphs and tribulations. In the ascent to success, victories may be celebrated, and accolades may abound. But as the winds of fortune change, so too can the landscape of prosperity shift. It is during these moments that leaders must possess the courage to confront the stark reality that their once-thriving business is now navigating treacherous waters.

This is not a journey for the faint of heart, for confronting the truth requires a rare blend of emotional intelligence and business acumen. It is the willingness to peer into the mirror of accountability, to see with unclouded eyes the decisions made, and the consequences that followed. Here, leaders are faced with a choice – to retreat into the shadows of denial or to step boldly into the crucible of reality.

To admit that your business is in trouble is not an admission of failure, nor a pronouncement of doom. Rather, it is a pivotal moment in the narrative of leadership, where humility takes the reins and guides the course of action. In the face of adversity, true leaders rise above ego and embrace the vulnerability that comes with acknowledging fallibility.

Creating an environment of open communication is the cornerstone of this transformative process. The leaders who truly inspire are those who foster a culture where every team member feels empowered to voice their concerns and ideas without fear of judgment. In such an ecosystem, authenticity thrives, and creativity blossoms.

During times of crisis, transparency emerges as a vital asset. The tendency to shield employees from unsettling truths may be tempting, but it is a disservice to the very people who form the backbone of the organization. When employees are kept informed about the challenges the company faces, they become stakeholders in the journey towards recovery.

Transparency nurtures trust, and trust becomes the currency that fortifies teams during tumultuous times. In moments of uncertainty, it is not just the grand proclamations of leaders that resonate but their willingness to reveal vulnerability. By acknowledging their own concerns and fears, leaders create a safe space for others to do the same, thus weaving the tapestry of a resilient and tightly knit workforce.

This commitment to honesty and vulnerability is the catalyst that galvanizes the collective spirit, propelling the company forward in unison. It ignites the spark of innovation, inspiring teams to seek ingenious solutions to the challenges at hand. Through open communication, employees can contribute ideas without restraint, feeling secure in the knowledge that their voices are valued, and their insights appreciated.

Confronting the truth is a hallmark of exceptional leadership. It is the pivot upon which the trajectory of a troubled business can be altered. Admitting that your business is in trouble is not an admission of weakness, but a declaration of strength – a strength that emanates from humility, self-awareness, and the commitment to face adversity with candor and courage.

It is through this transformation that a business finds resilience to weather storms and the wisdom to navigate uncharted waters. When leaders dare to embrace the truth, they illuminate a path of hope and redemption, guiding their teams towards a brighter, more prosperous future.

Analyzing the Root Causes: Understanding What Led to the Downfall

In the chronicles of business history, the downfall of once-thriving enterprises has often been a cautionary tale, a solemn reminder of the importance of continuous introspection and adaptation. When a business finds itself on the precipice of failure, it is not enough to merely acknowledge the grim reality. True leaders understand that the path to redemption lies in the unyielding pursuit of understanding – understanding the root causes that led to the unraveling of their once-flourishing vision.

The process of analyzing the root causes is not for the faint of heart. It demands a willingness to navigate the labyrinth of decisions, strategies, and executions that culminated in the current situation. It calls for an unvarnished assessment of the actions taken, the risks embraced, and the consequences borne.

This introspective journey must be undertaken with rigor and honesty, for superficial analyses and half-hearted examinations will yield little fruit. It is a task that must involve all relevant stakeholders and departments, for a single misstep in any area can send shockwaves that reverberate throughout the entire organization.

At times, this pursuit of understanding may unearth uncomfortable truths, revealing vulnerabilities and shortcomings that may have been concealed in the allure of success. The temptation to assign blame or engage in finger-pointing may arise, but true leaders resist such inclinations. Instead, they foster an environment that encourages accountability without condemnation, where mistakes are acknowledged, and growth is prioritized over punishment.

Every failure, no matter how catastrophic, holds within it the seeds of growth and transformation. It is here, amidst the ruins of the past, that leaders can sow the seeds of a more resilient and successful future. To learn from the mistakes that led to the downfall is to harvest wisdom from adversity.

The objective is not to absolve oneself or others of responsibility, but to illuminate the path to redemption. As leaders confront the uncomfortable truths that emerge, they must strive to identify areas for improvement with clarity and precision. This process may necessitate difficult decisions and fundamental changes to the organization's structure, culture, or direction.

The spirit of growth and evolution must permeate every facet of this analysis. The past is an invaluable teacher, but only if its lessons are heeded and integrated into the fabric of the company's DNA. Leaders must encourage a growth mindset, where every setback is viewed as an opportunity for refinement, and every obstacle becomes a steppingstone towards progress.

In this pursuit of understanding, leaders may find solace in knowing that they are not alone. History is replete with stories of renowned leaders and visionary entrepreneurs who faced adversity and emerged stronger. From their experiences, leaders can draw inspiration and wisdom, realizing that even the most extraordinary journeys are replete with moments of trial and tribulation.

Analyzing the root causes that led to the downfall of a business is a defining chapter in the narrative of leadership. It is an introspective journey that requires courage, humility, and a commitment to learning from the past. True leaders resist the temptation to assign blame and instead seek to understand the underlying factors that contributed to the challenges faced.

Through this process, leaders lay the foundation for a more resilient and successful future, one that embraces growth and adapts to the ever-changing landscape of business. In the crucible of analysis, leaders unearth the precious gems of wisdom that propel their organizations forward, casting aside the shadows of failure and embracing the radiance of transformation.

The Importance of Objectivity: Making Tough but Necessary Decisions

In the melting pot of challenging times, leaders find themselves navigating treacherous waters, where emotions can rage like tempests, threatening to drown out reason and clarity. In these turbulent moments, the importance of objectivity emerges as a beacon of light, guiding leaders through the storm towards a calmer shore. It is through the lens of objectivity that tough but necessary decisions can be made, decisions that steer the ship of the company towards the greater good and ensure its survival in the face of adversity.

Objectivity is the antidote to the intoxicating mix of emotions that can cloud judgment and hinder progress. As leaders confront the trials that beset their business, it becomes paramount to step back from the tempestuous sea of feelings and adopt a clear and unbiased mindset. The ability to detach personal feelings from the realm of business decisions is an invaluable skill that separates exceptional leaders from those led astray by sentimentality.

One of the most arduous tasks a leader may encounter is evaluating the effectiveness of the current team and making the tough decision to enact personnel changes. Restructuring the team may be a necessity to realign with the company's new direction and strategy. However, this must be undertaken with fairness and empathy, acknowledging the contributions of every individual while recognizing that change is an inevitable part of growth and survival.

In the pursuit of objectivity, leaders must tread delicately, mindful of the impact that personnel decisions can have on both the organization and the individuals involved. Empathy becomes a companion to objectivity, fostering an understanding of the human element that underlies each decision. It is through compassion and sensitivity that leaders can guide their teams through periods of transition and change, preserving morale and cohesion amidst uncertainty.

In addition to personnel matters, leaders must also subject the company's offerings, market position, and overall business model to a rigorous reassessment. The landscape of commerce is ever evolving, and staying relevant and competitive demands a willingness to adapt to new market trends and changing customer demands.

Objectivity, in this context, becomes a navigational tool that steers leaders away from the shores of complacency. It empowers them to confront realities with an unflinching gaze, to recognize when cherished practices or products may no longer serve the company's objectives. The ability to pivot, to shed the old and embrace the new, becomes an emblem of resilience and foresight.

Throughout this process of decision-making, communication emerges as a lifeline that keeps the crew united and informed. Leaders must ensure that every member of the team understands the reasoning behind the decisions and the vision for the future. Transparency becomes the cornerstone of trust, as open dialogue bridges the divide between leaders and their workforce.

As the ship sails towards uncharted waters, empathy and understanding help to ease the transition, dispelling fears and fostering a sense of camaraderie. In times of uncertainty, a united front emboldens the company to weather the storm together, fortifying each member to face challenges with determination and resolve.

The importance of objectivity in making tough but necessary decisions cannot be overstated. It is the rudder that steers leaders through emotional tempests, enabling them to chart a course that serves the greater good of the company. Objectivity empowers leaders to evaluate their teams, assess their strategies, and adapt to changing circumstances with resilience and grace.

Through transparency, empathy, and clear communication, leaders build a culture of trust and understanding that weathers the storms of change. In this crucible of objectivity, leaders pave the way for a future that is not only sustainable but also flourishing, driven by the wisdom and strength that comes from making tough but necessary decisions.

CHAPTER 2

ASSESSING VIABILITY
CAN YOUR BUSINESS BE SAVED?

Can Your Business Be Saved?

The process of reviving a struggling business is one that necessitates a multi-faceted approach, with the first and arguably the most important step being an honest assessment of the business's viability. The ability to survive and thrive in the business landscape is contingent on numerous factors, with financial stability being significant, but by no means, the only determinant. The organization's adaptability, its market position, and its core competencies also play a pivotal role. This chapter will provide a deep dive into the key elements required in assessing business viability and the means by which one can make an informed decision about the future of their business.

The primary objective of a viability assessment is to identify the core issues negatively impacting the business, and to evaluate whether these issues can be remedied within the

constraints of the existing framework. A detailed analysis is required, encompassing the financial, operational, market, and strategic dimensions of the business.

The first checkpoint of a viability assessment involves a

detailed examination of the financial health of the business. This includes scrutinizing balance sheets, income statements, and cash flow statements to understand the business's fiscal standing better. Identifying trends in revenues, costs, profitability, and cash flow will provide insight into the business's financial stability or instability.

A common pitfall in this step is the tendency to focus solely on short-term liquidity issues without considering the underlying causes of these problems. Solving a cash flow issue may provide temporary relief, but a viable business must demonstrate long-term financial sustainability. Hence, it's crucial to analyze long-term solvency ratios, profitability margins, and financial leverage.

A business's operational efficiency is integral to its viability. A thorough operational review should delve into the intricacies of the organization's supply chain, production processes, HR, sales and marketing, and customer service.

Identifying inefficiencies or bottlenecks can help elucidate why the business is underperforming. For instance, a business might be plagued by low productivity, high employee turnover, poor customer service, or outdated production methods. Addressing these operational issues could be the key to turning the business around.

Understanding the market dynamics and your position within the market is an indispensable part of assessing a business's viability. A thorough market evaluation includes understanding the competitive landscape, the changing consumer behavior, market trends, and the regulatory environment.

A successful business should ideally cater to an existing market need or be flexible enough to adapt to emerging trends. If the market for a product or service is shrinking or the competition is too fierce, it may be time to consider a pivot.

Finally, the strategic assessment analyzes whether the

business's current strategy aligns with its mission, vision, and the market conditions. It requires an introspective look at the core competencies of the business and whether they can be leveraged for a competitive advantage.

Strategic evaluation also includes an examination of the business's leadership. Effective leadership can steer a struggling business toward success, while a lack of clear leadership can result in business failure.

After conducting these assessments, business owners will have a holistic understanding of their business's state. If the problems identified are fixable and the business has a clear path to profitability and growth, the business may indeed be viable. If the challenges are insurmountable, or the necessary changes are not feasible, it may be time to consider other options such as selling, merging, or even liquidating the business.

The path forward after a viability assessment depends on the specific circumstances of the business. However, with a detailed, honest, and comprehensive evaluation, business owners will be well-equipped to make informed decisions about the future of their business.

Evaluating the Feasibility of a Turnaround

Regardless of the severity of a business crisis, not all companies can be salvaged. The process of turning around a struggling business is, after all, a feat that necessitates significant resources, time, and expertise. Therefore, before investing in any recovery efforts, a critical prerequisite is to assess the feasibility of a turnaround. This chapter will guide you through the salient features of this evaluation process,

elaborating on key factors such as financial health, market analysis, operational efficiency, leadership and talent, and brand reputation.

The financial status of a company is a clear indicator of its wellbeing and ability to survive hardships. To ascertain the feasibility of a turnaround, it's essential to conduct a detailed analysis of the company's financials.

Scour the financial statements, cash flows, and debt obligations to understand the financial position and risks. Key performance indicators like profit margins, debt-to-equity ratio, and return on investment should be considered. Simultaneously, look for unsustainable financial practices, such as consistent borrowing for operational expenses, that may hinder a successful recovery. If the business cannot project profitability or maintain positive cash flow in the foreseeable future, the feasibility of a turnaround might be questionable.

The next critical phase in this assessment is a robust market analysis. Understanding the current dynamics of your industry and your company's position within that landscape can illuminate the pathway towards recovery.

Start by examining the competitive landscape to identify the unique selling propositions of competitors and how your offerings compare. Look for gaps in the market that your business can fill. Analyzing customer trends can provide insights into shifts in preferences, giving a window to tweak your offerings. Potential growth opportunities, like emerging market trends or underserved market segments, can be the lifeline your business needs. If your analysis shows a hostile market environment with scarce growth opportunities, the prospects of a turnaround might be grim.

Operational efficiency often serves as the backbone of a successful business. During this stage of evaluation, you need to take a deep dive into the company's internal processes, production capabilities, and supply chain management.

Identify operational bottlenecks, inefficiencies, and areas that bleed resources. This process can be as granular as scrutinizing production line efficiency, or as broad as assessing supply chain resilience. Pinpointing areas of inefficiency could pave the way for cost-saving measures, vital for the turnaround process. If inefficiencies are rampant and systems are outdated with limited scope for improvement, the feasibility of a turnaround could be at stake.

A ship is only as good as its captain. For a business, the leadership team and the talent pool play a significant role in shaping the company's future. Hence, a critical evaluation of the management team's skills, expertise, and their ability to steer the company out of a crisis is crucial.

Look for leaders who can inspire, manage change effectively, and have a track record of making tough decisions under pressure. If the current team lacks these capabilities, you may need to consider bringing in fresh talent or engaging a turnaround consultant. If finding or affording such talent is out of reach, it may hamper the turnaround process.

Finally, understanding the company's brand image and reputation in the market is key. A brand with a strong reputation and loyal customer base can weather the storm more effectively than one with a tarnished image.

Assess the company's reputation through customer feedback, online reviews, and market surveys. If the brand image is severely damaged or customer loyalty is waning, reviving the brand might require a significant investment in terms of resources and time.

In conclusion, evaluating the feasibility of a turnaround is an exercise in realism. It demands a careful, comprehensive, and brutally honest analysis of various facets of the business. Only when the business shows promise across all these factors can a turnaround be deemed feasible. Otherwise, it might be wise to consider alternative routes such as restructuring, merger, sale, or in extreme cases, liquidation. Remember, the goal is not merely survival but sustainable growth and success in the long run.

Seeking Expert Advice: Engaging Consultants and Specialists

While resilience and ingenuity are invaluable attributes for any business leader steering their company through tumultuous times, one must also recognize when to enlist external help. The path towards business recovery is fraught with complexity and challenges that often require a specialized set of skills and experience. Hence, engaging consultants and specialists can be a game-changing move in the turnaround journey. This chapter will offer a comprehensive guide to seeking expert advice and making the most of their expertise.

Before you set out on your search for a specialist, it is crucial to understand your specific needs. This involves taking stock of the situation and identifying areas that require expert intervention.

These areas could be diverse, ranging from financial restructuring, marketing and branding strategies, operational efficiencies, to technological upgrades. The key here is to recognize where your current team may lack the necessary skills or resources. Recognizing these gaps will help narrow down the type of consultant or specialist your business requires.

Once the needs are identified, the next step involves seeking potential consultants or firms specializing in those areas. Conducting thorough research is essential at this stage.

Leverage your professional network, industry associations, or digital platforms like LinkedIn for recommendations. Look for consultants with a successful track record in turnaround management, particularly those who've handled businesses of a similar size and industry. Review their qualifications, experience, and areas of specialization.

Based on these criteria, create a shortlist of potential consultants or consulting firms that align with your business's needs.

After shortlisting potential consultants, it's time to delve deeper into their understanding of your business's challenges and their proposed solutions. Interviews provide a platform for this exploration.

Ask them about their approach to the identified problem areas and potential solutions. Discuss their previous experiences in similar situations and their understanding of your business and industry. Gauge their ability to think strategically, their adaptability to unexpected changes, and their willingness to work closely with your team. Their responses will provide you with insights into their competence and compatibility with your business.

Lastly, validate the information gathered during the interviews by checking references. Contacting previous clients can provide first-hand accounts of the consultant's effectiveness, professionalism, and ability to deliver results.

Inquire about their work ethics, punctuality, ability to meet deadlines, and their success in driving desired outcomes. Such feedback is crucial in assessing whether the consultant or the firm can indeed offer the value they promise.

Seeking expert advice is an investment—one that could potentially change the course of your business. But like all investments, it demands due diligence, careful selection, and constant evaluation. By following these steps, you can ensure you're bringing in the right experts to drive your business towards a successful turnaround. Remember, while consultants bring their expertise, the final decisions rest with you, the business leader. Your ability to leverage their insights while staying true to your business's core values and vision is what will ultimately define the success of your turnaround strategy.

Weighing the Risks and Benefits: Determining the Best Path Forward

In the world of business, decisions are rarely black and white. Each choice presents a unique blend of risks and benefits, particularly when one stands at the precipice of a business turnaround. This delicate balancing act demands a thoughtful approach. It requires assessing potential risks, performing cost-benefit analysis, understanding the time sensitivity, and seeking input from stakeholders. This chapter will explore each of these considerations in depth, providing a guide to navigating this complex decision-making process.

Embarking on a turnaround journey is akin to navigating a ship through stormy seas. There will be challenges and potential risks that can take many forms – financial, operational, or even reputational.

Financial risks could include escalating costs or potential losses associated with the proposed changes. Operational risks may entail disruptions to your supply chain or resistance to changes within the workforce. Reputational risks involve the potential backlash from customers or a tarnished brand image due to drastic changes.

Identifying these risks early on allows for proper planning and risk mitigation strategies. The process involves anticipating potential obstacles and strategizing on how to prevent, minimize, or respond to these challenges.

Once the risks are understood, a cost-benefit analysis is in order. This involves a meticulous evaluation of the projected costs of implementing a turnaround plan versus the potential benefits of a revitalized and profitable business.

The costs are not merely financial; they could involve time, effort, and potential opportunity costs. The benefits, on the other hand, while primarily financial, could also include improved market positioning, operational efficiencies, and a more engaged workforce.

If the benefits substantially outweigh the costs, and you have the resources to bear these costs, it bolsters the case for a turnaround. Conversely, if the costs are too high with minimal benefits, it might be time to consider other alternatives.

The turnaround process is a race against time. The longer the business continues its downward trajectory, the harder and more costly the recovery will be. Therefore, consider the urgency of acting and the impact of the delay on the company's prospects for recovery.

However, while swift action is crucial, it's equally important not to rush into decisions without adequate planning and assessment. Striking the right balance between timeliness and careful deliberation is key.

Last, but far from least, is the importance of involving key stakeholders in the decision-making process. Stakeholders could include employees, board members, investors, creditors, or even key customers. Each brings a unique perspective to the table, and their buy-in is crucial for the successful implementation of the turnaround plan.

Engage them early and often, communicate the challenges openly, and seek their input. This not only enhances the decision-making process but also builds support for the chosen path forward.

Determining the best path forward for a struggling business is not a task to be taken lightly. It requires meticulous analysis, foresight, and courage. By weighing the risks and benefits, considering the time factor, and involving stakeholders, you can ensure that your decision is not just an instinctive reaction, but a strategic move designed to steer your business towards sustainable success.

CHAPTER 3

CUTTING LOSSES
MAKING DIFFICULT BUT VITAL CHANGES

Cutting Losses: Making Difficult but Vital Changes

When a business teeters on the precipice of implosion, making difficult but vital changes becomes an imperative, not a choice. Whether the cause is fierce competition, outdated business models, market disruptions, or internal inefficiencies, the need for decisive, swift, and often painful action is unavoidable. This process—commonly referred to as "cutting losses"—can entail everything from staff reductions and divestment of underperforming assets to reimagining business strategies and redefining corporate identities.

First, we must address the elephant in the room: the people. Cutting losses often means downsizing—reducing the workforce. This is one of the most painful decisions a leader has to make. It involves taking away livelihoods, disrupting lives, and potentially creating feelings of mistrust and disillusionment among the remaining workforces. Yet, when survival is at stake, it's a step that may be necessary. It is critical that leaders handle such processes with utmost care, compassion, and transparency, ensuring that the affected employees receive support to make their transition easier.

Another form of loss cutting involves the sale or closure of underperforming or non-core business units. These might be product lines that are no longer profitable, divisions that no longer align with the company's strategic direction, or assets that are draining resources without delivering adequate returns. While divesting these parts of the business can be disruptive and may involve additional short-term costs, it can free up resources and allow the organization to focus on areas that offer better prospects for growth and profitability.

However, loss cutting is not only about reducing costs. It's also about strategic shifts that can save a business on the brink of collapse. This might involve reimagining the business model, pivoting towards more lucrative markets, or investing in innovative products or services that offer potential for future growth.

Consider, for instance, the case of LEGO. In the early 2000s, the iconic toy company was on the verge of bankruptcy. It was struggling with huge losses, largely due to overdiversification into areas such as theme parks and clothing lines. LEGO's turnaround strategy involved making tough decisions to cut losses—it divested non-core assets, streamlined operations, and laid off a substantial part of its workforce. But crucially, LEGO also reconnected with its core business—building sets that stimulated creativity and imagination. By focusing on its unique strengths and its loyal customer base, LEGO managed to turn the tide and is now a profitable, thriving business.

In a similar vein, cutting losses may involve changing entrenched mindsets and processes within the company. Businesses on the verge of implosion often suffer from deep-rooted cultural or operational issues that need to be addressed. This could involve breaking down bureaucratic silos, fostering a more innovative and risk-taking culture, or replacing outdated technology and inefficient processes with more efficient and agile ones.

In conclusion, cutting losses is a complex, multi-faceted process that involves making hard decisions, confronting uncomfortable truths, and forging a new path. It's about reducing costs, yes, but it's also about more than that. It's about strategic shifts, cultural transformation, and a relentless focus on the core strengths and values that can steer a faltering business back to solid ground. In the face of impending implosion, it's not just about survival—it's about building a foundation for sustainable, future success.

Streamlining Operations: Identifying Inefficiencies and Waste

Efficiency—the concept of achieving maximum productivity with minimum wasted effort or expense—has become the lifeblood of modern organizations. Streamlining operations is more than a business trend; it is a necessity for survival in an era of ceaseless competition, rapid technological advancement, and escalating customer expectations.

Inefficiencies are like sand in the gears of a finely tuned machine. They impede progress, contribute to wear and tear, and ultimately, cause breakdowns that can bring an entire operation to a standstill. However, the first step to eliminating these inefficiencies is identifying them. This calls for an unwavering commitment to meticulous scrutiny of every facet of the organization: departments, processes, workflows, and more.

The process begins with each department. An exhaustive review of roles, tasks, and results can illuminate areas of redundancy or under-utilization. Similarly, deep dives into specific processes can identify steps that add little or no value to the outcome or product. Such granular investigation will likely reveal inefficiencies that have been accepted as part of the status quo but are leeching valuable resources without corresponding returns.

A critical aspect of this discovery process is fostering a culture that not only encourages but celebrates open communication. This means establishing an environment where employees at all levels feel safe to voice their opinions, share their ideas, and highlight inefficiencies they perceive in their day-to-day work. This bottom-up communication can prove invaluable. After all, who better to spot a problem than those on the front lines?

However, the identification of inefficiencies is not a task to be carried out solely by human intuition and perception. The role of data in this endeavor cannot be understated. In today's digital world, nearly every action leaves a digital footprint—a trove of data waiting to be analyzed. Advanced technologies, such as artificial intelligence (AI), machine learning, and predictive analytics, can sift through these vast datasets and detect patterns or anomalies that may point to potential inefficiencies.

For instance, if customer service call times have been increasing, AI-powered analytics can delve into the data to find out why. Are agents spending too much time on certain types of calls? Are there recurring issues that could be resolved at the source, reducing the number of calls entirely? Data provides the evidence needed to objectively identify areas that need improvement.

Once inefficiencies have been identified, the process of streamlining can begin. Streamlining is not merely about cutting costs—it's about refining processes to create a leaner, more agile organization. It's about doing more with less and doing it better. It means eliminating redundancies, automating routine tasks, optimizing resource utilization, and continuously striving for improvement.

In the end, a streamlined organization is one that is primed for success. It is an organization that has the flexibility to pivot when needed, the agility to seize opportunities when they arise, and the resilience to weather whatever challenges the business landscape may throw its way. It is an organization that is not merely surviving but thriving amidst the relentless tides of change. And in today's world, that's not just a goal—it's an imperative.

Downsizing vs. Restructuring: Choosing the Right Approach

Choosing the most suitable approach for effecting change in an organization—downsizing or restructuring—can be a complex decision with far-reaching implications. Both strategies have their place in the business toolbox, each with its unique advantages and potential drawbacks. As leaders steer their organizations through the turbulent waters of change, they must consider not only immediate financial outcomes but also the long-term sustainability and cultural implications of their choices.

Downsizing, also known as "rightsizing," is often the first strategy that comes to mind when an organization needs to reduce costs quickly. It involves trimming the workforce and/or selling off non-essential assets, such as underperforming divisions or unnecessary property holdings. The immediate benefits can be substantial: reduced payroll, lower overhead costs, and improved cash flow, which can all serve to enhance the company's financial health in the short term.

However, the downside of downsizing is as steep as its upside is swift. Downsizing can take a severe toll on the organization's human capital—the morale, engagement, and productivity of the remaining workforce. Layoffs can engender fear, resentment, and uncertainty among survivors, leading to reduced productivity, lower job satisfaction, and increased turnover. Additionally, companies that downsize may find themselves short-staffed when business conditions improve, potentially incurring significant rehiring and retraining costs.

Contrast this with restructuring—a strategic effort to realign the organization's structure and operations to better meet its business objectives. Restructuring can encompass a range of measures, from departmental reorganization and process redesign to the redistribution of roles and retraining of employees.

Unlike downsizing, restructuring does not necessarily involve cutting headcount. Instead, it focuses on optimizing the allocation of resources—people, processes, and technology—to enhance productivity and efficiency. The aim is to create a leaner, more agile organization that is better equipped to meet its strategic objectives.

Restructuring, though, is not without its challenges. It requires a comprehensive, meticulous analysis of the organization and its operations. It demands time, resources, and commitment from both leadership and staff. Moreover, restructuring can also lead to uncertainty and anxiety among employees, particularly if communication is mishandled or if the changes are not well understood.

Despite these potential pitfalls, restructuring often offers a more sustainable path forward. By focusing on improving operations rather than merely reducing costs, restructuring can enhance the organization's competitiveness and long-term viability. Moreover, by involving employees in the process and providing opportunities for retraining and growth, restructuring can help preserve—and even boost—employee loyalty and motivation.

Choosing between downsizing and restructuring is a decision that should not be taken lightly. Leaders must weigh the short-term financial benefits of downsizing against the potential harm to employee morale and the long-term sustainability of their business. They must also consider the time, effort, and resources required for a successful restructuring and the impact it may have on their workforce and operations.

The best approach will depend on the unique circumstances and strategic objectives of each organization. Regardless of the chosen path, however, it is crucial that leaders communicate transparently with their employees, address their concerns, and involve them in the change process. After all, it is the people—their skills, creativity, and dedication—that ultimately drive the success of any organization.

Preserving Core Values: Retaining the Essence of Your Business

In the tumultuous currents of change, whether driven by downsizing, restructuring, or other strategic shifts, an organization's core values are its anchor. These foundational principles—integrity, commitment to customers, innovation, or any other values that the company holds dear—serve as the guiding lights that shape its identity, culture, and strategic direction. Preserving these core values amidst transformation is paramount for maintaining brand loyalty, customer trust, and organizational cohesion.

When an organization fails to protect its core values during times of change, it risks losing more than just its identity—it risks compromising the very essence that makes it unique and valuable to its stakeholders. Customers, employees, and other key stakeholders may feel disillusioned or alienated if they perceive the organization to be veering from its guiding principles.

Therefore, aligning any organizational changes with the company's mission, vision, and long-term goals is essential. These strategic guideposts should serve as the compass by which the organization navigates the sea of change. Any proposed changes should be evaluated not just on financial or operational metrics, but also on how well they align with these core elements.

Leaders play a pivotal role in preserving core values during periods of transition. They must embody these values in their actions and decisions, even when making tough calls. Equally important, they must communicate openly and transparently with all stakeholders—employees, customers, investors, and others—about the rationale for the changes, how they align with the company's core values, and the expected outcomes.

By communicating clearly and proactively, leaders can help to dispel fear and uncertainty, foster understanding, and build trust. They can also mitigate resistance to change and limit negative reactions by assuring stakeholders that, while certain aspects of the organization may evolve, its essence—the values and principles that define its identity—will remain intact.

A study of businesses that have successfully navigated significant changes while preserving their core values can provide illuminating insights and practical lessons. Companies such as IBM and Netflix, for instance, have undergone dramatic transformations in their business models and operations without losing sight of their core values. IBM pivoted from a hardware-focused business to a leader in cloud computing and AI, all while maintaining its commitment to innovation, trust, and responsibility. Netflix transitioned from a DVD rental service to a global streaming powerhouse, yet its core values of judgment, communication, curiosity, and courage remained steadfast.

By examining such case studies, readers can gain valuable insights into how these businesses managed to change their strategies, operations, and structures without compromising their essence. These stories serve as potent reminders that while companies must evolve and adapt to survive, they must also remain true to their core values—their heart and soul.

Preserving core values amidst transformation is a balancing act—one that requires vision, courage, and tenacity. But those who succeed will emerge from the crucible of change not only to be stronger and more resilient but also true to who they are. And in an ever-changing business landscape, authenticity and consistency can be a company's most valuable assets.

CHAPTER 4

RECONNECTING & REBUILDING TRUST
REVIVING BRAND PERCEPTION

The old adage "a chain is only as strong as its weakest link" has profound implications in the world of business. If you imagine a business as a chain, the links represent the various aspects that hold the organization together - its processes, people, products, services, and most critically, its customers. This chain, when solid and well-maintained, can bear the weight of the most strenuous of business challenges. Yet, any negligence in maintaining the integrity of these links, especially the one with customers, could compromise the entire structure.

As businesses grapple with the pressure to survive and thrive amidst intense competition and evolving market conditions, they often have to make tough decisions. These decisions might involve downsizing, restructuring, or other significant operational changes that can strain the chain's strength. Amidst these challenging times, it's easy for businesses to become internally focused - to concentrate on cost-cutting, streamlining operations, and improving efficiency. While these internal modifications are necessary,

It's paramount not to neglect the chain's most vital link - the relationship with customers.

Addressing customer concerns and complaints in a timely and efficient manner is critical to maintaining the strength of this link. More than just resolving the issue at hand, it's about empathizing with the customer's situation, acknowledging their frustration, and reaffirming their value to your business. Remember the adage: people don't care how much you know until they know how much you care.

Consider the case of Zappos, the online shoe and clothing retailer, known for its exemplary customer service. They believe in going above and beyond to address customer concerns. The company once even helped a customer find a local pizza delivery place when she couldn't find any that were still open. This customer-centric approach not only resolves issues but also builds a lasting connection with customers, strengthening that critical link.

Another aspect of maintaining the strength of the customer link is the ability to adapt to their changing needs. Businesses must keep a pulse on these shifts in customer preferences, understanding that what worked yesterday might not work today, and what works today might not work tomorrow.

Take the case of the music industry. With the advent of the internet, music consumption patterns began to change dramatically. Some companies clung to the old model of selling albums and saw their fortunes decline. Others, like Spotify, recognized this shift and adapted to the new demand for streaming music, thereby successfully capturing a substantial market share.

During challenging times, a brand's perception can take a hit. However, through transparent communication, effective reputation management, and a commitment to corporate social responsibility, businesses can revive their brand's perception, thereby reinforcing that critical link.

An excellent example of this is Johnson & Johnson's handling of the Tylenol crisis in the 1980s. Their swift, transparent, and ethical response to the crisis not only saved the Tylenol brand but also enhanced the overall brand perception of Johnson & Johnson, strengthening their link with customers.

In the world of business, as in chains, resilience is key. It's about acknowledging the importance of each link and ensuring none are neglected, especially the link with customers. As businesses navigate the turbulent waters of tough decisions, it's crucial not to lose sight of the customer, to respond swiftly to their concerns, adapt to their changing needs, and manage the brand's perception. By doing so, they can ensure their chain remains robust and resilient, capable of withstanding whatever business challenges come their way. After all, a chain is only as strong as its weakest link, and in business, there is no link more vital than the one with customers.

Addressing Customer Concerns and Complaints

The cornerstone of any successful business is its customers. These relationships, however, are not without their challenges. At some point, every business will face customer complaints—a seemingly negative experience that, when managed correctly, can provide invaluable insights into the inner workings of a company's products, services, or processes.

When businesses face challenging circumstances, an uptick in customer concerns or complaints is often a natural consequence. However, this influx of feedback should not be seen as a burden; rather, it represents an opportunity to improve and adapt. Acting swiftly, responding empathetically, and crafting effective solutions to these concerns can help preserve and even strengthen customer trust during these critical periods.

Effective complaint resolution starts with active listening. This involves more than just hearing the words a customer is saying. It requires an effort to understand the underlying emotions and intentions behind those words.

When a customer presents a complaint, businesses should ensure they have the full picture before responding. This means allowing the customer to fully express their grievances without interruption or defensiveness. Active listening also involves acknowledging their feelings and empathizing with their experience.

A classic example of active listening can be found in the customer service strategies of Zappos, the online shoe retailer known for its exemplary customer care. In a culture where call center operatives are often encouraged to keep call times short, Zappos empowers its representatives to spend as long as necessary on a call to ensure the customer feels heard and their concerns are fully understood.

Once a complaint is fully understood, the next step is to provide an effective response. This usually involves some form of solution—be it a product replacement, a refund, or a service correction. However, the delivery of this solution is just as important as the solution itself.

At this stage, empathy is key. It's not enough to simply offer a solution; the customer must also feel valued and cared for throughout the process. The goal is not just to resolve the problem, but also to leave the customer with a positive impression of how their complaint was handled. This is an opportunity to turn a potentially negative experience into a moment of delight that deepens the customer's relationship with the brand.

Consider the case of the Ritz-Carlton. The luxury hotel chain allows its employees to spend up to $2,000 per day to improve a guest's experience or solve a problem. This level of autonomy not only empowers employees but also ensures that guests feel genuinely valued, as problems are solved quickly and effectively.

In the final analysis, addressing customer concerns and complaints is more than just problem-solving—it's about transforming potentially negative situations into opportunities for improvement and connection. By actively listening, responding with empathy, and providing effective solutions, businesses can turn customer complaints into valuable feedback, deepen relationships, and build lasting trust.

By adopting such an approach, businesses can turn challenging circumstances into catalysts for growth and improvement, reinforcing customer trust and loyalty in the process. It's not just about resolving issues—it's about building stronger, more resilient relationships with the very people who drive the business: the customers.

Reviving Brand Perception: Strategies for Effective Reputation Management

In times of great upheaval, a company's reputation often bears the brunt of the storm. As the sea of business churns, it's all too easy for brand perception to be negatively affected. But even amidst these turbulent times, businesses can employ savvy strategies to manage and even revive their brand's standing. This delicate dance of reputation management rests on the pillars of communication, utilization of various media channels, and commitment to corporate social responsibility.

Reputation management begins and ends with communication. During a crisis or period of significant change, a company's silence can be its downfall. In the absence of clear information, speculation and rumors can run rampant, causing considerable damage to the company's reputation. Businesses must strive for transparency, communicating regularly about the current situation, actions being taken, and the expected outcomes.

Consider the case of Johnson & Johnson during the Tylenol crisis in the 1980s. When the company's product was tampered with, leading to several deaths, the company acted swiftly and transparently. They removed 31 million bottles of Tylenol from the shelves, costing them more than $100 million. They kept the public informed every step of the way, thus retaining public trust despite the crisis.

In our hyperconnected world, businesses have a multitude of channels at their disposal to communicate their messages. Traditional media such as press releases, news conferences, and print advertisements still play a vital role. However, they should be used in conjunction with digital channels like social media platforms, email newsletters, and corporate blogs to create a well-rounded communication strategy.

Engaging with influencers and key opinion leaders in the industry can help amplify positive messages and aid in shaping public perception. These individuals, with their significant follower bases, can add credibility and a wider reach to the company's narrative.

Starbucks provides an excellent example of utilizing diverse media channels to address a crisis. In 2018, following an incident where two black men were unjustly arrested at a Philadelphia Starbucks store, the company immediately responded by closing more than 8,000 stores for a day to conduct racial-bias training. They used traditional and social media channels to communicate their actions and commitment to addressing the issue.

Lastly, demonstrating corporate social responsibility is a powerful tool for repairing a tarnished brand image. Ethical behavior, community involvement, and environmental sustainability are no longer just 'nice to have' but expected from businesses by consumers. Actions that show genuine commitment to these areas can strengthen brand perception and foster goodwill among stakeholders.

One classic example is Patagonia, the outdoor apparel company. It has a long-standing reputation for environmental activism and ethical business practices. From donating 1% of sales to environmental causes to encouraging customers to repair their gear instead of buying new, Patagonia's commitment to corporate social responsibility significantly enhances its brand perception.

In conclusion, managing and reviving brand perception during tough times is a multifaceted endeavor. But through transparent communication, strategic use of diverse media channels, and an unwavering commitment to corporate social responsibility, businesses can weather any storm, emerging with a reputation that is not only intact but potentially even stronger than before. The storms of business are inevitable, but with the right strategies, companies can not only survive these storms but use them as opportunities for growth and improvement.

Focusing on Customer Needs: Adapting to Changing Demands

A key determinant of success in the ever-evolving business landscape is a business's ability to recognize, anticipate, and adapt to shifting customer needs. An organization's longevity hinges on its ability to not merely react to changes in the marketplace, but to proactively identify emerging trends and pivot accordingly. Understanding customer needs, preferences, and desires is at the heart of this ability to adapt.

Keeping Your Finger on the Pulse of Change. Market research, customer feedback, and social listening tools serve as the lifeblood of customer insight. Together, they can reveal valuable data about emerging trends, evolving customer preferences, and unfulfilled needs.

In-depth interviews, focus groups, and customer surveys can provide direct insights into what consumers want and need. Social listening tools, on the other hand, monitor online conversations and social media platforms to capture real-time sentiment about a brand and its competitors.

Take, for example, the case of LEGO, the renowned toy manufacturing company. Faced with near bankruptcy in the early 2000s, LEGO turned to market research and customer feedback to understand what consumers really wanted. This led to the development of new, successful product lines based on popular franchises, like Star Wars and Harry Potter, effectively reviving the brand.

Innovation is the key to adapting, however, understanding customer needs is just the first step. Businesses must be nimble enough to respond to these insights with innovation in their products, services, and processes. This could mean tweaking an existing product, overhauling a service, or even radically shifting the business model.

Look at Netflix as an example. Initially a DVD-by-mail service, Netflix understood the changing needs and preferences of its customer base and pivoted towards streaming services, and eventually, creating original content. Today, it's hard to imagine a world without Netflix originals like "Stranger Things" or "The Crown."

Ultimately, the goal of all these efforts is to deliver value in a way that resonates with customers' evolving needs and expectations. Businesses should aim to not merely meet customer expectations but to exceed them. In doing so, they can create strong customer loyalty and set themselves apart from the competition.

Apple is a company that's mastered this approach. It continually innovates and creates products that don't just meet customer needs but anticipate them. The introduction of the iPhone wasn't simply about fulfilling a need for a smartphone—it was about revolutionizing how we interact with technology.

The business landscape may be turbulent, but those who can navigate these waves are the ones who never lose sight of the customer. They understand that, at its core, business is about relationships.

By studying businesses that have successfully navigated these challenges, we can learn valuable lessons. These insights can serve as a compass guiding other businesses on their journey. After all, in the business world, it's often the relationship with customers that determines whether a business sinks or swims. And those who place the customer at the center of all they do are those best positioned to swim, no matter how rough the waters get.

CHAPTER 5

INNOVATION AND ADAPTATION
PIVOTING FOR SUCCESS

Business isn't a fixed entity; it's a fluid, ever-evolving organism. In this competitive and dynamic landscape, the ability to pivot—making substantial modifications to a company's business model—is vital for ongoing success.

Pivoting can take multiple forms: it might involve introducing new products or services that better serve customer needs or even create new ones; shifting focus to different consumer segments as demographics, preferences, and societal trends evolve; adopting innovative technologies to enhance efficiency, product quality, or customer experience; or altering operational practices to optimize resource allocation or meet new regulatory standards.

Every successful pivot begins with recognizing the need for change. That recognition could stem from declining sales figures, a novel technology that threatens to disrupt the industry, or a shift in consumer behavior. However, perceiving the need for change isn't sufficient, companies must also have the courage to enact that change, even when it involves venturing into uncharted territory and leaving behind established practices.

For an illustrious example of successful pivoting, we need to look no further than IBM, a technology behemoth whose history dates back over a century. IBM—short for International Business Machines—did not start as the computing giant we know today. The company's origins lie in the manufacture of punch card systems, used for data processing in the pre-computer age.

As technology advanced, IBM continued to adapt and evolve. From punch card systems, the company transitioned to mainframe computers, then to personal computers, and then to software and services as the tech industry continued to mature and transform. Today, IBM is a global leader in fields as diverse as artificial intelligence, cloud computing, and consulting services.

What makes IBM's journey truly remarkable is its willingness and ability to reinvent itself time and again, regardless of its existing success. The company did not merely react to changes in the industry; it anticipated those changes and adapted proactively. IBM's success story is a testament to the power of the pivot: the ability to change course, not as a last-ditch effort to survive, but as a strategic move to thrive.

As we delve deeper into the concept of pivoting, we will explore the nuances of this strategy, the signs that indicate a pivot may be necessary, and the practical steps to execute a successful pivot. Drawing from real-world examples like IBM, we will illustrate the transformative potential of the pivot, showcasing its power to redefine companies, rejuvenate brands, and reshape industries.

Embracing Change: Encouraging a Culture of Innovation

The world of business is a crucible where only the most adaptable can thrive. The ability to innovate and adapt is no longer a luxury; it's a necessity for survival. To keep pace with rapid technological progress, changing consumer preferences, and fierce competition, businesses must foster a culture of innovation—a culture that embraces change and sees it not as a threat, but as an opportunity for growth, for improvement, and for new possibilities.

This culture of innovation should not be confined to a specific department or a small group of designated "innovators." It must permeate every level of the organization, influencing every decision, every process, and every interaction. This innovative spirit must be imbued in the company's DNA.

A culture of innovation starts at the top. Leaders must not only talk about innovation but also demonstrate it through their actions. This includes encouraging new ideas, no matter how outlandish they may initially seem, promoting a willingness to experiment, and displaying a readiness to take calculated risks. At the same time, they need to foster an environment where failure is seen not as a catastrophe but as a learning opportunity, a steppingstone on the path to success.

Google, the global technology giant, is a prime example of a company that has fostered a powerful culture of innovation. Known for its pioneering "20% time" policy, Google encouraged its employees to spend 20% of their time pursuing their own innovative projects, separate from their regular work. This policy was not merely a perk; it was a strategic move to unlock creativity, foster innovation, and keep employees engaged.

This approach led to the creation of some of Google's most successful and transformative products, including Gmail, Google News, and AdSense. By institutionalizing innovation, Google ensured a steady stream of fresh ideas and continued to push the boundaries of technology, transforming the way we live and work in the process.

However, fostering a culture of innovation is not just about implementing creative policies. It's about creating an atmosphere where people feel safe to share their ideas, where collaboration is encouraged, where diversity is celebrated, and where everyone feels they have a stake in the company's future. In such an environment, innovation thrives, and the company can continually reinvent itself to stay at the cutting edge of its industry.

As we delve further into this topic, we will explore in-depth how companies can foster a culture of innovation, examining successful policies and initiatives from industry leaders, discussing the role of leadership in encouraging innovation, and providing practical tips for promoting an innovative mindset at every level of the organization.

Identifying Opportunities: Exploring New Markets and Product Lines

In business, as in nature, it often adapts or perishes. As markets evolve, technologies advance, and consumer needs and tastes change, companies must be ready to identify and seize new opportunities. This may involve exploring new markets, developing new product lines, or reimagining existing ones. But the journey into the unknown is a complex and challenging endeavor. It requires not only deep insight and understanding of market trends and consumer behavior but also creativity, foresight, and the courage to venture beyond the familiar.

Market research is the compass that guides this journey. Through meticulous research, companies can identify emerging trends, understand evolving consumer preferences, and spot gaps in the market that represent potential opportunities. But it's not enough to understand the current market landscape. Businesses must also anticipate where the market is heading and position themselves to meet the needs of tomorrow, not just today.

Creativity is the fuel that propels this journey forward. It allows businesses to see beyond what currently exists and imagine what could be. It helps them identify unmet needs, conceive new solutions, and design innovative products that not only meet but exceed customer expectations.

Netflix, the global streaming giant, exemplifies the power of identifying and seizing new opportunities. The company began as a DVD rental service, competing with the likes of Blockbuster. But as the internet became more pervasive and bandwidth increased, Netflix saw an opportunity. It pivoted to offering a streaming service, providing customers with on-demand entertainment in the comfort of their homes.

But Netflix didn't stop there. With a keen understanding of its audience and a forward-looking view of the market, it identified another opportunity: producing original content. This move, seen as risky at the time, has paid off handsomely. Netflix's original shows and movies have not only won critical acclaim and attracted a global audience but also set the company apart from its competitors, solidifying its position as an industry leader.

As we delve deeper into this topic, we will examine how businesses can effectively identify and capitalize on new opportunities. We will explore the tools and techniques for conducting effective market research, discuss strategies for fostering creativity and innovation, and provide insights on how to manage the risks and challenges associated with venturing into new markets or developing new product lines. Through real-world case studies and practical advice, readers will gain valuable insights and strategies to help their businesses adapt, innovate, and thrive in the ever-changing business landscape.

Learning from Competitors: Gaining Insights to Stay Ahead

In the race for business supremacy, competitors are not merely rivals to outperform but sources of valuable knowledge. Observing their moves, understanding their strategies, and analyzing their outcomes can provide rich insights into what works and what doesn't. There's a wealth of learning in both their triumphs and their tribulations.

Indeed, observing competitors' successes can spark inspiration, helping businesses identify successful strategies and practices that can be adapted to their own context. For instance, a competitor's innovative product feature or customer service approach might inspire a business to experiment with similar ideas, while tweaking them to align with their own brand and value proposition.

More importantly, the missteps and pitfalls competitors encounter on their journeys offer powerful lessons in what to avoid. It's much less costly to learn from others' mistakes than to make them yourself. A careful analysis of where competitors have gone wrong can help businesses steer clear of similar pitfalls and make more informed decisions.

Take, for example, the upheaval in the mobile phone industry triggered by the advent of smartphones. For years, companies like Nokia and BlackBerry dominated the mobile phone market with their feature phones and QWERTY devices. However, when Apple introduced the iPhone in 2007, it marked the dawn of a new era in mobile technology. The smartphone, with its touch screen interface and multitude of apps, quickly became the new standard in mobile communication.

Yet, established players like Nokia and BlackBerry were slow to adapt to this change. Their inability to let go of their successful past and embrace the future proved disastrous, leading to a sharp decline in their market share. On the other hand, newcomers like Apple and Samsung, who were not shackled by legacy products, quickly seized the opportunity. They understood the shift in consumer preferences and delivered products that met these new demands, swiftly rising to dominate the smartphone market.

This tale of technological disruption underscores the importance of learning from competitors. Had Nokia and BlackBerry been more alert to the moves of their competitors and more responsive to the changing market dynamics, they might have been able to better navigate the shift to smartphones. Their story serves as a stark reminder to businesses of the importance of keeping a close eye on the competition and being ready to adapt and evolve.

In this chapter, we delve deeper into the strategies and techniques for effective competitor analysis. We explore how to extract meaningful insights from competitors' successes and failures and how to use this knowledge to inform your own business strategy. Through practical examples and case studies, we illustrate the power of learning from competitors to stay ahead in the fast-paced and ever-changing business landscape.

Navigating the Path to Success

The path to business success is seldom a straight line. It's a winding road that demands agility, foresight, and a willingness to take calculated risks. Companies that have managed to scale the heights of success and sustain their momentum over time are those that have embraced innovation and adaptation as integral parts of their business strategy.

Innovation isn't just about creating new products or services. It's about challenging the status quo, questioning existing assumptions, and exploring novel ways to deliver value. It's about pushing boundaries, breaking new ground, and continuously striving to improve and evolve. It's about fostering a culture that encourages creativity and risk-taking, where employees feel empowered to experiment, learn, and grow.

But innovation in isolation isn't enough. It needs to be accompanied by a readiness to adapt—to evolving market conditions, emerging customer needs, technological advancements, and competitive pressures. Successful companies are those that can sense changes in their environment and swiftly respond, making strategic shifts and recalibrations to align with the new reality.

Consider, for instance, Amazon. The e-commerce giant

started as an online bookstore but quickly expanded to offer a vast range of products, recognizing the potential of the e-commerce market. It later ventured into cloud computing with Amazon Web Services, now a multi-billion-dollar business and a major profit driver for the company. More recently, Amazon has made strides into the realm of artificial intelligence with products like Alexa. The company's relentless focus on innovation and its ability to pivot in response to market opportunities have been key to its phenomenal success.

This journey towards innovation and adaptation isn't easy. It's fraught with uncertainty and risk. There will be failures along the way. But as the saying goes, the only real failure is the failure to try. Companies that learn from their missteps, that see failure as a steppingstone to success, are the ones that can navigate the path to success

In the end, it's about having the courage to dream big, the wisdom to plan well, and the tenacity to persevere. It's about building an organization that is resilient, agile, and relentlessly customer focused. It's about embracing change, not as a threat, but as an opportunity to learn, grow, and break new ground.

In this dynamic and ever-evolving world of business, it is the companies that innovate and adapt, that dare to chart their own course, that will rise to the top, outshine the competition, and redefine the rules of the game.

CHAPTER 6

FINANCIAL RECOVERY
ENSURING SUSTAINABLE GROWTH

"From Survival to Sustainable Growth" encapsulates the journey that a business must undertake as it recovers from financial hardship or near-implosion. There is a stark difference between merely staying afloat and charting a course for ongoing, sustainable growth. The former is about enduring the present; the latter is about designing the future. It is, undeniably, an uphill journey, often presenting a multitude of challenges that test the resilience of an organization. Yet, it is through this arduous journey that businesses evolve, becoming more robust, adaptable, and, eventually, sustainable.

Financial stability lies at the heart of this transformation. Stability is not merely the absence of volatility; it is a condition that allows a business to withstand future shocks. The pursuit of stability requires diligence, keen oversight, and strategic decision-making, as organizations must dissect their financial health, identify weaknesses, and work relentlessly to fortify those areas.

But financial recovery isn't solely about damage control. It involves actively managing debts and renegotiating with creditors to ease immediate pressures. It is about asserting control over the financial future of the company, adopting sound budgeting practices that marry realism with ambition, and ensuring resources are allocated effectively.

While it is crucial to put out the fires, businesses should not lose sight of the forest. The goal of financial recovery is not just to survive the crisis at hand, but to set the stage for sustainable growth. It's about building a business that can thrive in the long term, that can navigate uncertainties and seize opportunities, and that can create enduring value for its stakeholders.

Throughout this chapter, we will delve deeper into each of these aspects. We will offer practical strategies drawn from real-world examples, featuring companies that have not just survived financial crises, but have emerged stronger and more resilient. Each of these stories presents valuable insights, offering a roadmap for businesses embarking on their recovery journey.

The path from survival to sustainable growth is neither linear nor predictable. It's a journey marked by challenges, setbacks, learnings, and victories. It demands resilience, adaptability, and a relentless focus on the future. But the reward – a stronger, more sustainable business – is well worth the effort. After all, it is often through surviving the most challenging storms that businesses become truly unshakeable.

Restoring Stability

The process of restoring stability is akin to steadying a ship in turbulent waters. It's a critical stage in the journey to financial recovery, requiring a keen eye, steady hands, and above all, a clear understanding of the situation at hand.

This process begins with a comprehensive assessment of the business's financial health. This isn't merely a matter of number crunching; it's a systematic investigation to uncover the root causes of financial distress. To do this, businesses need to dissect their balance sheets, income statements, and cash flow statements. They must scrutinize assets and liabilities, evaluate revenue streams, and dissect cost structures. They should probe for inefficiencies, bottlenecks, and vulnerabilities, with the aim of identifying problem areas that are putting pressure on the financial health of the company.

The key to this assessment is honesty. It's about confronting the harsh realities that might have been ignored or overlooked in better times. This can be a difficult process, especially for businesses that have a long-standing history or emotional attachment to certain products, services, or practices. However, it's an essential step towards understanding the financial situation and making informed decisions for recovery.

With a clear understanding of financial health, businesses can then move to the next critical step – stemming the bleed. This isn't about quick fixes or band-aid solutions. It's about taking decisive, strategic actions that halt the downward spiral and stabilize the business.

These actions can take various forms, depending on the specific challenges and circumstances of the business. For some, it might mean cutting non-essential expenses, streamlining operations, or improving efficiencies. For others, it might involve divesting underperforming assets, renegotiating contracts, or reorganizing the business structure. Some businesses might have to consider more drastic measures, such as layoffs or closure of certain branches.

While these decisions can be tough, they're necessary for the long-term health and stability of the business. They're about making choices that might be painful in the short term, but that set the stage for recovery and future growth.

It's important to remember that restoring stability is not a one-time exercise. It's a continuous process, requiring ongoing oversight, regular assessments, and course corrections. It's about maintaining a steady hand on the tiller, keeping a watchful eye on the horizon, and navigating the business through the storm towards calmer waters. In the next sections, we'll delve deeper into the specific strategies and tactics that businesses can adopt in this journey.

The Road to Financial Health: Implementing Sound Budgeting

As businesses regain stability and set their sights on a more financially secure future, it becomes paramount to implement a comprehensive and effective budgeting strategy. Establishing sound budgeting practices can serve as the backbone of a robust financial recovery plan, providing a roadmap to navigate the treacherous waters of financial distress.

A well-crafted budget offers multiple benefits. It creates a framework for allocating resources judiciously, helping to ensure that every dollar is put to its best possible use. It sets clear financial targets, establishing benchmarks for revenues, expenses, profits, and cash flows that provide tangible goals for the organization to aim for. Furthermore, it provides a basis for monitoring financial performance, allowing the business to track its progress and make course corrections as necessary.

Despite its apparent simplicity, budgeting is far from a straightforward task. It requires a deep understanding of the business's operations, market dynamics, and financial capabilities. It calls for careful forecasting of revenues and expenses, considering factors such as sales trends, price changes, economic conditions, and competitive pressures.

Moreover, effective budgeting is not a one and done exercise. It's an ongoing process that should be regularly reviewed and updated to reflect the changing business environment and performance. This could be a quarterly or even monthly exercise, depending on the volatility of the business environment and the pace of change within the organization.

In addition to being a regular exercise, the budgeting process should be a collaborative effort. It should involve input from all areas of the business - from sales and marketing to operations and finance. This ensures a holistic view of the business, incorporating diverse perspectives and fostering a sense of ownership and accountability across the organization. It also helps to create a more realistic and achievable budget, grounded in the realities and constraints of the business.

By following these principles, businesses can create a sound budget that provides a clear financial roadmap for the journey ahead. It can help them navigate the twists and turns of the recovery process, ensuring that they stay on the path to financial health and sustainable growth. As we continue our exploration of financial recovery strategies in the following sections, we'll delve into more detail on how to implement these budgeting practices effectively.

Negotiating with Creditors: Managing Debt and Liabilities

Businesses grappling with financial distress often find themselves burdened by substantial debts and liabilities. Whether these stem from loans, supplier credit, lease obligations, or other sources, they can exert significant pressure on a business's cash flow and financial stability. In such situations, one crucial step towards recovery is managing and, if necessary, restructuring these debts and liabilities. This is where the art of negotiation comes into play.

Negotiating with creditors can be a daunting task. It requires a deep understanding of your financial situation, a clear plan for recovery, and the communication skills to convey this effectively to your creditors. However, it's essential to remember that creditors usually have a vested interest in your business's survival. After all, they stand to lose if the business fails and is unable to repay its debts. This shared interest can provide a starting point for negotiation.

The first step in this process is to conduct a thorough review of your debts and liabilities. Understand the terms of your loans, the interest rates, the payment schedules, and any penalties or charges for late payment or default. Identify the most pressing debts - those with the highest interest rates, the most stringent terms, or the largest outstanding balances.

Once you have a clear picture of your debts, develop a realistic repayment plan. This plan should take into account your current financial situation, your projected cash flows, and your overall recovery plan. It should set out how much you can afford to repay, how frequently, and over what period.

Armed with this information, approach your creditors to negotiate more favorable terms. This might involve seeking a reduction in interest rates, an extension of the repayment period, a temporary pause on repayments, or even a partial forgiveness of the debt. It's crucial to approach these negotiations with transparency, providing clear evidence of your financial situation and explaining your recovery plan.

In these discussions, present your proposed repayment plan, demonstrating how it aligns with your recovery strategy and future cash flows. Show your creditors that you are committed to repaying your debts and that you have a viable plan to do so. Provide regular updates on your progress, maintaining open lines of communication throughout the recovery process.

Remember, negotiations may not always result in the ideal outcome, and it may take time to reach an agreement. But even small concessions can help ease the financial strain, giving your business more breathing room to recover and grow.

As we continue in this chapter, we'll delve deeper into the strategies and techniques for successful debt negotiation, drawing on real-world examples and expert advice to provide a comprehensive guide for businesses navigating the tricky path to financial recovery.

Creating a Cash Flow Strategy: Ensuring Sustainable Growth

As we navigate the intricacies of financial recovery, it's essential to keep our eyes on the horizon. The end goal isn't merely to weather the storm but to emerge stronger, more resilient, and primed for growth. One pivotal factor that can make or break this journey is the management of cash flow. After all, cash flow is the lifeblood of any business. It's what keeps the lights on, pays the bills, fuels investment, and underpins growth. So, how can businesses create a robust cash flow strategy to ensure sustainable growth?

A well-crafted cash flow strategy begins with meticulous tracking of income and expenditure. Understand where your money is coming from and where it's going. This isn't limited to your primary sources of income and regular operational expenses. Consider secondary income streams, indirect costs, seasonal variations, and irregular expenses. The more granular your understanding, the better you can manage your cash flow.

Next, manage your receivables and payables effectively. On the receivables side, this means having robust policies for credit control, invoicing, and collections. Aim to minimize the time between providing a product or service and receiving payment for it. On the payables side, negotiate favorable terms with suppliers and creditors, taking advantage of any discounts for early payment and avoiding penalties for late payment. However, be careful not to stretch your suppliers too far, as this could strain relationships and disrupt your supply chain.

Maintaining a cash buffer is another key aspect of a strong cash flow strategy. No matter how well you manage your income and expenses, unforeseen circumstances can and do arise. Having a cash buffer can be the difference between weathering these surprises and being capsized by them. While the size of the buffer may vary depending on the nature and size of your business, it should be sufficient to cover any unexpected expenses or shortfalls in income.

Finally, cash flow forecasting is crucial. Predicting future cash inflows and outflows enables you to anticipate cash shortages, plan for investment, and identify opportunities for growth. These forecasts should be based on realistic assumptions about your business performance and the wider market conditions. They should also be updated regularly to reflect changes in these variables.

Creating a robust cash flow strategy isn't a one-off task. It's an ongoing process that requires constant vigilance, regular review, and timely adjustments. It might seem daunting, but the reward is a solid financial foundation that not only supports recovery but also fuels sustainable, profitable growth.

As we conclude this chapter on financial recovery, we must remember that the journey doesn't end here. Financial recovery is just one piece of the puzzle. True recovery encompasses every facet of the business, from operations and marketing to human resources and strategy. It's about rebuilding, reinventing, and reimagining the business for a new era. In the chapters to come, we'll delve deeper into these aspects, providing a comprehensive guide to business recovery in a post-crisis world.

CHAPTER 7

RESILIENCE IN LEADERSHIP
FROM SURVIVING TO THRIVING

From Surviving to Thriving

The transition from mere survival to genuine thriving in the corporate landscape is a journey of resilience, perseverance, and unyielding spirit. During a crisis, a business can become akin to a ship tossed on stormy seas, and in these tumultuous times, it is the leaders who step up as the navigators, guiding their organizations through the storm towards safer, prosperous waters. In this chapter, we dissect the nuanced, crucial elements that define resilience in leadership, focusing on inspirational leadership, the power of leading by example, the importance of transparent communication, and strategies to nurture employee morale.

Crises, for all their disruptions, also present extraordinary opportunities for transformation. They act as agents of change, compelling businesses to rethink, reimagine, and retool their strategies. They foster a sense of urgency and focus, stripping away complacency and business-as-usual thinking. It is in these crucibles of change that innovation, growth, and evolution are born. And this transformation is not a process that happens to the business; rather, it's one that's led by the business - specifically, by its leadership.

Leadership, in the face of crisis, evolves from mere

management to a beacon of hope, a source of reassurance, and a catalyst for change. The leaders' actions, their decisions, their attitude, and most importantly, their resilience, can spell the difference between succumbing to the crisis or emerging from it stronger and better equipped for the future.

The role of leadership in crisis goes beyond strategic decisions and tactical moves. It extends to the realm of emotions and attitudes, shaping the collective psyche of the organization. Leaders are tasked with not just navigating the business complexities of the crisis but also managing its human aspects. They need to inspire their teams to keep going, instill confidence amidst uncertainty, uphold morale in the face of adversity, and foster a sense of unity and shared purpose.

In this chapter, we explore the facets of resilient leadership. We delve into how leaders can inspire their teams to believe in the possibility of a brighter future, even when the present seems bleak. We look at the power of leading by example, where leaders reflect the resilience, positivity, and determination they want their teams to emulate. We delve into the necessity of transparent communication, where leaders keep their teams informed, engaged, and involved, reinforcing trust and cohesion. And we examine the importance of nurturing employee morale, where leaders recognize efforts, celebrate wins, and create a supportive, collaborative environment.

In the face of crises, businesses do not have the luxury of choosing whether or not to change. Change is inevitable. The real choice lies in the manner of this change - whether to passively endure it or actively guide it. And this choice rests largely with leadership. Through resilience and determination, leaders can steer their organizations from merely surviving crises to thriving despite them, and ultimately, because of them. The road might be challenging, but the destination - a stronger, more resilient, more innovative business - is worth the journey.

Inspiring the Team

Great leadership isn't just about managing; it's about inspiring. In the face of adversity, a resilient leader must step up and rally their team with more than just business strategy and logical tactics. Inspiration is the spark that ignites determination, fosters unity, and empowers teams to navigate through challenging times. An inspiring leader motivates their team to transcend their current circumstances, fostering a shared vision that empowers them to work towards a collective goal with passion, commitment, and an unwavering belief in their ability to prevail.

To inspire their teams, effective leaders tap into the power of storytelling. They frame the company's journey as a narrative, weaving together its history, its struggles, its triumphs, and its aspirations into a compelling story. This narrative, carefully articulated and sincerely conveyed, helps the team understand their place within the broader context of the company's journey. It reinforces their sense of purpose, enhancing their engagement and commitment to the company's mission.

Moreover, resilient leaders paint a picture of the future that stirs optimism and excitement. They position the crisis not as a disaster that brings operations to a halt, but as a challenge that can be surmounted and an opportunity that can lead to growth and innovation. They talk about the potential waiting to be unlocked, the opportunities on the horizon, and the success that lies beyond the immediate crisis. This forward-looking perspective breeds hope, keeping the team motivated and focused despite the hardships they may be facing.

These leaders also cultivate a belief in the team's collective strength and abilities. They show faith in their team's capacity to handle adversity and solve complex problems. They remind their team members of their past successes, their unique skills, and the value they bring to the organization. This affirmation boosts the team's confidence and nurtures their resilience, empowering them to face challenges head-on.

Inspiring leadership also means demonstrating vulnerability. Resilient leaders do not shy away from expressing their own anxieties or doubts. Instead, they share their feelings honestly and openly, creating a safe space for their team members to do the same. This vulnerability fosters trust and encourages open dialogue, strengthening team cohesion and mutual support.

Resilient leadership is about creating a spark that ignites a fire of inspiration within the team. It's about motivating and galvanizing the team to come together, face challenges head-on, and work towards their shared goals with determination and resolve. By doing so, resilient leaders lay the foundation for their teams to rise above the crisis and pave the way for future success.

Leading by Example: Maintaining Positivity and Determination

Resilient leaders understand the power of their own actions and attitudes. Their behavior, more than any speech or directive, sends a powerful message to their team. If they wish to instill positivity and determination within their team, they must first embody these qualities themselves. They must lead by example, offering a living model of the attitudes and behaviors that can enable the team to persevere through the crisis and emerge stronger on the other side.

Positivity in leadership isn't about presenting an artificially rosy picture of the situation or brushing aside the challenges at hand. Instead, it's about maintaining a solutions-oriented mindset, even when faced with daunting problems. It's about framing challenges as opportunities for learning and growth, rather than insurmountable obstacles. This positive approach encourages the team to focus on what they can do rather than what they can't, fostering a proactive and optimistic mindset that fuels problem-solving and innovation.

Moreover, a positive leader acknowledges the difficulties and uncertainties but simultaneously highlights the potential and possibilities. They celebrate small victories, appreciate individual contributions, and remind their team of their collective strength and shared purpose. This infusion of positivity uplifts the team spirit, inspires hope, and reinforces their resilience, helping them to endure through the tough times.

Determination, on the other hand, is about steadfastness and tenacity. It's about relentlessly pursuing the company's objectives, despite setbacks and obstacles. A determined leader shows up every day, ready to tackle the challenges, no matter how hard the previous day was. They are the last to lose hope, the first to rise after a fall, and the one who keeps pushing when others are ready to throw in the towel.

Such leaders personify the mantra "fall seven times, stand up eight". They demonstrate unwavering commitment to their vision and their team. Their steadfastness and refusal to give up in the face of adversity serve as a powerful inspiration for their team, encouraging them to exhibit the same level of determination and perseverance.

By leading through positivity and determination, resilient leaders set the tone for their organization. They model the way, inspiring their teams to mirror these qualities and fostering a culture of resilience that permeates every level of the organization. This, in turn, equips the team to navigate through adversity, seize opportunities, and work collectively towards recovery and growth.

Transparent Communication: Keeping Employees Informed and Engaged

One of the defining traits of resilient leadership is transparent communication. When a crisis hits, the natural human response is to seek out information to understand the situation better and to alleviate uncertainties. If leaders fail to provide clear and accurate information, the vacuum can quickly be filled with rumors, speculation, and misinformation, which only serve to heighten anxieties and create confusion.

Resilient leaders understand the importance of keeping their teams informed through frequent and honest communication. They provide regular updates about the situation, the steps being taken to address the issues, and the progress being made. They don't shy away from sharing bad news, understanding that the team can handle hard truths better than uncertainty.

But transparency isn't just about relaying information top-down. It's also about opening channels for dialogue, encouraging questions, listening to concerns, and inviting suggestions. By fostering a two-way communication culture, resilient leaders not only ensure that their team members feel heard and valued but also tap into a wide range of perspectives and ideas that could help navigate the crisis.

Furthermore, transparent communication fosters trust. When leaders communicate openly, they demonstrate that they respect their team enough to share the truth, even when it's hard. This strengthens the bond of trust between the leader and the team, enhancing their collective resilience.

Finally, transparent communication helps keep employees engaged during turbulent times. When team members are informed and feel involved in the process, they are more likely to stay focused and committed to their roles, contributing positively to the organization's recovery efforts.

In essence, transparent communication is about fostering an environment where information flows freely, where questions are encouraged, and where every voice is heard. It's about cultivating a culture of openness and trust, ensuring that the entire team remains aligned, informed, and ready to face the challenges together. By doing so, resilient leaders not only navigate their team through the crisis but also lay the foundation for a more open, inclusive, and resilient organizational culture going forward.

Nurturing Employee Morale: Encouraging Teamwork and Support

The final component of resilient leadership revolves around nurturing employee morale. It's an inescapable fact - crisis periods are strenuous. They bring uncertainty, induce anxiety, and test the team's resilience. In such trying times, maintaining high employee morale becomes vital. It is the fuel that keeps the team going, enabling them to face challenges head-on and persist in their efforts toward recovery.

Resilient leaders understand the importance of nurturing morale. They know that the success of the recovery effort is directly tied to the motivation and commitment of their team. Therefore, they take deliberate steps to boost morale and create an uplifting work environment.

One effective way of doing this is by recognizing and acknowledging the team's hard work. A simple 'thank you' or 'good job' can go a long way in showing team members that their efforts are seen and valued. Celebrating small victories, even when the bigger goal is still distant, can also provide a much-needed morale boost. It gives the team a sense of progress and reassures them that their efforts are moving the company in the right direction.

Moreover, resilient leaders understand the importance of support during these times. They are approachable, ready to listen, and quick to provide help when needed. They create an environment where team members feel comfortable voicing their concerns or asking for help, reinforcing the message that they're all in this together.

Encouraging teamwork is another strategy that resilient leaders employ to nurture morale. A crisis is a collective challenge, and therefore, it requires a collective response. By promoting collaboration, leaders not only distribute the workload but also foster a sense of camaraderie and mutual support. Teamwork creates a shared sense of purpose and ownership, reinforcing the idea that everyone has a role to play in the recovery journey.

In the face of adversity, a team that works together, supports each other, and shares a belief in their collective strength is a formidable force. It amplifies the team's resilience, as they draw strength from each other's hope and determination. And as they navigate the storm together, they forge bonds that will see them through not only the current crisis but future challenges as well.

In conclusion, resilient leadership is a multifaceted concept that encompasses inspiring the team, leading by example, communicating transparently, and nurturing morale. It's not a trait that leaders are born with, but a skill that can be developed with intention and practice. And as we've seen, it can make all the difference on the recovery journey, turning a disparate group of individuals into a cohesive, resilient team, poised to overcome any challenge and seize every opportunity that comes their way. This is the power and promise of resilience in leadership.

CHAPTER 8

STRATEGIC PARTNERSHIPS
LEVERAGING RESOURCES

Businesses, much like the people behind them, are inherently social entities. They exist and flourish within an ecosystem of relationships, interactions, and collaborations, drawing strength from their connections and networks. Strategic partnerships, therefore, become a vital pillar of this ecosystem, allowing businesses to unlock unprecedented opportunities for growth, innovation, and competitive advantage. They provide the framework for collective action, collaboration, and mutual success, extending beyond transactional relationships and paving the way for enduring alliances.

Strategic partnerships can bridge gaps in resources, expertise, or technology, allowing businesses to leverage each other's strengths and compensate for weaknesses. They can lead to shared innovations, co-created products, and joint ventures that might not have been possible for each business to achieve independently. They can expand a business's reach into new markets, tapping into the partner's established customer base or distribution networks. They can also provide a platform for learning, knowledge sharing, and talent development.

Strategic partnerships often begin with a clear understanding and appreciation of each partner's resources. These resources can be tangible, such as financial capital, physical assets, or technological infrastructure. They can also be intangible, such as brand reputation, market knowledge, customer relationships, or intellectual property. By pooling these resources, strategic partnerships can create synergies that amplify their combined value, resulting in greater efficiency, cost savings, risk sharing, or market dominance.

In addition to resource pooling, strategic partnerships can create unique collaborative opportunities. By aligning their goals and combining their skills, knowledge, and resources, partners can undertake joint projects, co-create innovative products, or enter new business domains. These collaborative initiatives can result in shared successes, foster deeper trust and understanding, and strengthen the partnership bond.

Partnerships can serve as a conduit to new markets, both geographical and sectoral. Partnering with a local business can provide an entrant with valuable insights into the local market dynamics, consumer behavior, regulatory landscape, and business practices. This can greatly reduce the time, cost, and risk associated with market entry. Similarly, businesses can enter new industry sectors through partnerships, leveraging their partner's industry expertise and networks.

Finally, strategic partnerships can contribute to building robust business networks. These networks can be a source of new partnerships, business leads, industry insights, investment opportunities, and talent acquisition. Effective networking involves active engagement, reciprocal value creation, and relationship nurturing. It's about building trust, demonstrating credibility, and fostering long-term relationships.

In conclusion, navigating the path to collaborative success involves strategically leveraging resources, creating collaborative opportunities, accessing new markets, and building robust networks. It involves choosing the right partners, nurturing partnership relationships, and creating shared value. It's about understanding that in the interconnected world of business, success is not a zero-sum game, but a collective endeavor, achieved not in isolation, but through collaboration and partnership.

Strategic Partnerships: Leveraging Resources

In the complex arena of business, the power to leverage resources through strategic partnerships is paramount. When resources are finite and competition is fierce, the intelligent utilization of mutual strengths can become the dividing line between thriving or merely surviving.

Strategic partnerships allow businesses to pool resources, creating a collective reservoir of tools, talents, and technologies that can be leveraged to achieve shared objectives. This practice is far from a simple exchange of resources; it is an alliance crafted from recognizing synergies, mutual needs, and complementary assets.

Tangible assets such as financial resources, equipment, and physical infrastructure are often the most evident resources to be shared. This exchange can lead to a reduction in operational costs as shared resources may eliminate the need for costly investments, thereby freeing up capital for strategic initiatives. Moreover, risk sharing is another considerable advantage, as partners can bear the financial and operational risks together, making large projects or investments more feasible.

Intangible assets, on the other hand, such as knowledge, expertise, intellectual property, and brand reputation can also be of significant value. Access to specialized knowledge or technology can expedite innovation, fuel growth, and provide a competitive edge in the market. For instance, a partnership between a start-up with an innovative product and an established company with a strong brand reputation and extensive distribution network can lead to successful market penetration for the start-up, while providing the established company with a novel product to diversify their offerings.

Further, leveraging resources in strategic partnerships can result in enhanced operational efficiency. With shared resources, partners can streamline processes, eliminate redundancies, and improve productivity. They can also learn from each other's best practices, thereby fostering continuous improvement and operational excellence.

In essence, the leveraging of resources in strategic partnerships is about synergy—the belief that the combined effort of the partnership will yield results greater than the sum of what each business could achieve individually. It is about seeking collaborative advantage in a competitive world, creating a win-win scenario that benefits all partners involved. This shared success can foster a sense of trust and mutual respect, forming the bedrock of a long-lasting and prosperous partnership.

Collaborative Opportunities: Forming Alliances with Complementary Businesses

Forming alliances with complementary businesses is like piecing together a complex jigsaw puzzle - the perfect fit can lead to a beautiful and powerful picture. Strategic partnerships offer a platform for businesses to collaborate, multiply their capabilities, and unlock potential growth opportunities that would be otherwise inaccessible.

The magic of these partnerships resides in the unique, symbiotic relationships that can arise from combining distinct yet compatible business elements. Collaboration between businesses that offer complementary products, services, or technologies can open the door to innovative possibilities, bridging gaps in offerings and providing customers with comprehensive solutions.

Take, for example, a business with niche technology but a limited customer base. By forming a strategic partnership with a business that has a broad customer network but lacks advanced technology, both can benefit. The first business expands its customer reach, while the second enhances its portfolio with cutting-edge technology.

Joint ventures present another form of collaborative opportunities. Two businesses might pool their resources and expertise to undertake a project or develop a product that neither could have accomplished alone. This fusion of strengths can lead to innovative outcomes, a wider range of services, and shared financial risk that can boost the confidence of the partners involved.

Additionally, alliances with complementary businesses can amplify market reach and penetration. A small business or start-up with an innovative product might lack the necessary resources or network to reach a large, dispersed audience. By partnering with a larger, well-established company that possesses extensive distribution networks, the smaller business can break through market barriers, getting their product in front of potential customers who were previously unreachable.

However, the formation of these alliances requires careful selection and due diligence. An in-depth understanding of each potential partner's strengths, weaknesses, and strategic objectives is crucial to ensure alignment. Furthermore, the groundwork for successful partnerships includes building trust, setting clear roles and expectations, and establishing efficient communication channels.

In essence, strategic alliances with complementary businesses can lead to a prosperous exchange of value, creating a synergy where the combined impact significantly outweighs the sum of individual efforts. This concept, often referred to as 'one plus one equals three,' signifies the profound potential these partnerships hold for mutual growth, innovation, and market expansion.

Accessing New Markets: Expanding Reach through Partnerships

The vast business landscape is dotted with numerous

markets, each offering distinct opportunities and challenges. For a company looking to extend its reach, strategic partnerships can be the compass guiding them towards untapped territories and new customer bases. Through alliances with established entities in desired markets, businesses can fast-track their market expansion journey, leveraging the local expertise, established customer relations, and distribution networks of their partners.

Partnerships can be particularly useful when venturing into international markets. The foreign terrain can be complex and challenging, fraught with unfamiliar customs, regulations, and consumer behaviors. Here, local partners act as the seasoned guides, navigating businesses through the maze of local market nuances. They bring to the table their deep understanding of the local culture, consumer preferences, and regulatory environment, making market entry less daunting and more strategic.

Imagine a business that has developed a revolutionary product, but its domestic market is saturated. By forming a strategic partnership with a company that already has a stronghold in a foreign market, the business can effectively extend its reach. It can take advantage of the partner's existing customer base, penetrate the market more rapidly, and build brand recognition under the umbrella of an already trusted local entity.

Such partnerships can also offer the advantage of an established distribution network. Trying to build a distribution network from scratch can be a costly and time-consuming endeavor, particularly in unfamiliar markets. However, a partnership with a local business can provide immediate access to distribution channels, expediting the product's path from factory to consumer.

Furthermore, strategic alliances can lower the financial risk associated with market expansion. Entering new markets can be a capital-intensive process, demanding significant investment in market research, localization of product offerings, and promotional activities. Partnerships can diffuse these costs, making market expansion a more affordable proposition.

However, while partnerships can provide a springboard into new markets, they also require careful planning and due diligence. It's essential to select partners that align with your brand values and strategic objectives and who possess a solid understanding of the local market landscape. Moreover, issues related to governance, profit sharing, intellectual property, and cultural differences need to be addressed upfront to ensure a fruitful and long-lasting alliance.

In conclusion, strategic partnerships, when navigated wisely, can be a powerful vehicle for market expansion. By connecting companies with new audiences, smoothing out distribution hurdles, and diffusing risk and costs, they can transform the intimidating journey into an adventure of exploration, discovery, and growth.

The Power of Networking: Building Connections for Mutual Benefits

In a world where 'who you know' often overshadows 'what you know,' the power of networking can be a game-changer. It's the invisible thread that weaves the business world together, connecting individuals, businesses, and ideas. Networks can be seen as the arteries of business, carrying opportunities, knowledge, support, and referrals. For businesses, this connectivity holds the promise of mutually beneficial relationships and prosperity.

Networking is not merely an exercise of attending industry events, making small talk, and exchanging business cards. It goes beyond these formalities, delving into the realm of genuine relationship building. Successful networking hinges on the development of meaningful and reciprocal relationships, founded on trust and mutual respect. It's not a one-way street, where one party benefits at the expense of the other. Instead, it's a symbiotic relationship, where the value flows both ways.

At its core, networking is about listening, sharing, and collaborating. It's about understanding the needs and challenges of others and offering solutions where you can. It's about sharing your own experiences, insights, and knowledge, and in return, learning from the experiences and perspectives of others. It's about creating an atmosphere of collaboration, where unique skills, perspectives, and resources are pooled together to create value greater than the sum of its parts.

Networking can also pave the way for strategic partnerships. When businesses connect, they uncover opportunities to complement each other's strengths, compensate for weaknesses, and create synergies. They can combine their resources and capabilities, innovate collaboratively, and jointly explore new markets. Such partnerships can lead to a significant competitive advantage, making the businesses more resilient and agile in the face of change.

Moreover, a robust network can attract the attention of potential investors, clients, and employees. Investors are more likely to invest in businesses recommended by their trusted networks. Clients, too, are more likely to trust businesses that are recommended by their peers. And talented professionals are drawn to businesses with a good reputation in the industry.

But perhaps the most important aspect of networking is the sense of community it fosters. In the volatile and competitive business landscape, having a network of trusted peers can provide emotional support, advice, and encouragement. It's a reminder that you are not alone on your business journey, and that there are others who understand your challenges and share your aspirations.

In conclusion, networking is more than just a business strategy; it's a way of navigating the business world. By building strong connections and fostering mutual benefits, businesses can tap into a wealth of opportunities and resources. Strategic partnerships and networking combined can serve as a beacon, guiding businesses through the fog of uncertainty towards uncharted territories and undiscovered opportunities. It's not merely about surviving but thriving amidst adversity and change. After all, as the African proverb goes, "If you want to go fast, go alone. If you want to go far, go together."

CHAPTER 9

LEARNING FROM MISTAKES
EMBRACING GROWTH

In the unforgiving world of business, where competition is fierce and margins for error are slim, mistakes are often viewed with trepidation. They are seen as costly missteps that can derail projects, tarnish reputations, and eat into profits. But this perspective, while understandable, only tells half the story. For, hidden within the gnarled roots of our mistakes, lies an invaluable source of learning, growth, and innovation.

Mistakes are the crucible in which resilience is forged and wisdom is distilled. They throw us into the deep end, pushing us out of our comfort zones and testing our mettle. They expose our weaknesses, highlight our blind spots, and reveal our true character. They humble us, reminding us of our fallibility and the transient nature of success. But most importantly, they teach us. They teach us about perseverance, humility, learning, and about growth.

Embracing this transformative power of mistakes requires a growth mindset. Coined by psychologist Carol Dweck, this term refers to the belief that our abilities and intelligence can be developed through dedication and hard work. A growth mindset encourages us to view challenges as opportunities for learning, effort as a path to mastery, and mistakes as steppingstones to success. It nudges us to shift our focus from outcomes to processes, from perfection to progress. When we embrace this mindset, we start seeing mistakes not as failures, but as feedback. We start viewing them not as setbacks, but as set-ups for future success.

Extracting valuable lessons from past missteps is another critical piece of the puzzle. It requires us to reflect on our actions, decisions, and their outcomes. It requires us to ask hard questions, seek honest feedback, and confront our shortcomings. It's about mining the depths of our mistakes, sifting through the debris of disappointment and regret, to unearth the nuggets of wisdom they contain. As we introspect and reflect, we begin to understand not just where we went wrong, but also why and how. This understanding equips us to make better decisions, take more informed risks, and ultimately, become better learners, leaders, and innovators.

Fostering a learning culture is a powerful strategy to harness the lessons from our mistakes. A learning culture is one that values curiosity, openness, and continuous improvement. It encourages individuals to take risks, make mistakes, and learn from them. It promotes a culture of feedback and learning, where every mistake is seen as a learning opportunity, every failure as a chance to grow. By fostering such a culture, businesses can increase their agility, resilience, and competitiveness. They can create a virtuous cycle of learning and improvement, fueled by the constructive use of mistakes.

Lastly, turning failures into steppingstones is about using setbacks to propel us forward. It's about reframing our narrative of failure, from one of defeat to one of learning and growth. It's about viewing every failure not as an obstacle, but as a steppingstone that brings us one step closer to our goals. And it's about leveraging our failures as catalysts for change, innovation, and progress.

In conclusion, the path to growth and innovation is not always smooth. It's a winding road, strewn with obstacles, setbacks, and mistakes. But as we embrace the growth mindset, reflect on our missteps, foster a learning culture, and leverage our failures as steppingstones, we begin to realize the transformative power of our mistakes. We begin to see that the journey to success is not about avoiding mistakes, but about learning from them. And we begin to understand that in the unforgiving world of business, it's not the mistakes that define us, but how we respond to them. For it's in our response that we find the seeds of growth, innovation, and success.

Embracing Growth

The concept of growth is intrinsically woven into the fabric of every successful business venture. However, it is crucial to understand that growth does not follow a clear, unobstructed, and upward trajectory. Rather, it traces a meandering path, punctuated by unexpected obstacles and setbacks. It is in navigating these challenges that the true essence of growth lies.

Embracing growth is about harboring a willingness to evolve, an openness to question established norms, and a readiness to venture into the unfamiliar. It requires a degree of vulnerability and a departure from the safe confines of the status quo. Most importantly, it necessitates the audacity to make mistakes and to view these not as failures, but as integral components of the growth journey.

The transition from fearing mistakes to learning from them marks a pivotal shift from a fixed mindset to a growth mindset, a concept coined by renowned psychologist Carol Dweck. In a fixed mindset, individuals perceive their abilities as static, shying away from challenges for fear of failure. Conversely, a growth mindset champions the notion that abilities can be developed over time through effort and perseverance. It encourages the embracement of challenges, viewing them as valuable opportunities to learn and grow.

This transformative shift from a pursuit of perfection to a pursuit of progress underlines the journey of embracing growth. Instead of obsessing over outcomes, focus pivots to the processes that drive these outcomes. The real triumph lies not in the ultimate success but in the relentless effort, the continuous learning, the resilience in the face of adversity, and the tenacity to rise above failure.

Mistakes, in this context, become invaluable steppingstones rather than insurmountable stumbling blocks. Every misstep becomes a lesson, every failure as a tutor. Each setback holds a mirror to areas of improvement, helping businesses and individuals to introspect, reassess, and reorient their strategies and efforts.

By embracing growth, challenges become steppingstones, effort becomes a conduit to mastery, and mistakes turn into invaluable lessons. This mindset fosters an environment of continuous learning, fostering resilience, encouraging innovation, and driving progress. In this realm, the focus rests not on the fear of falling but on the joy of rising each time we fall.

So, embrace growth. Embrace the challenges, the uncertainties, the mistakes. After all, these are the markers along the winding path of growth, signifying not our defeats, but our victories over fear, over stagnation, and over the past. And with each victory, we do not just grow; we evolve, becoming better versions of ourselves.

Extracting Valuable Lessons: Reflecting on Past Missteps

Past missteps, blunders, and mistakes can often feel like a blemish on our records - instances we would rather bury in the past and leave unmentioned. However, seen through the lens of a growth mindset, these mishaps are not blemishes but badges of honor, testament to the risks taken and the journey of learning embarked upon.

The process of extracting valuable lessons from past mistakes begins with reflection. This is not a mere casual backward glance at events gone by, but a rigorous and honest examination of our past actions and their outcomes. This act of reflecting is akin to turning the mirror on us, scrutinizing our decisions, and analyzing the path that led us to the end result.

Reflection necessitates asking tough, and often uncomfortable, questions. Why did a certain strategy not work? Where did our assessment go wrong? Were there warning signs we overlooked? Such introspection helps uncover hidden patterns, deep-seated biases, and faulty decision-making processes that might have contributed to the mistake.

Feedback from others, both from within the team and from external sources, can provide crucial outside perspectives. This external input can shed light on blind spots that may be invisible from our vantage point. It is essential to foster an environment where such constructive criticism is welcomed, and differing opinions are valued, as it fuels learning and facilitates improvement.

At the core of this reflective process is an acknowledgment of our shortcomings. It requires setting aside our ego, embracing humility, and admitting where we were wrong. It involves taking ownership of our mistakes, thus empowering us to rectify them.

The essence of reflection, however, is not merely to dwell on the past but to extract insights that can guide future actions. Every error carry within it a lesson to be learned. Whether it's a failed marketing campaign teaching us about our audience's preferences, a product recall underscoring the importance of quality control, or a botched negotiation highlighting the need for better preparation, each misstep provides valuable insights.

American philosopher and educational reformer John Dewey famously said, "We do not learn from experience...we learn from reflecting on experience." This adage holds particularly true in a business context.

Reflection turns experience into knowledge, mistakes into lessons, and the past into a tutor for the future.

In conclusion, extracting lessons from past missteps is not just about recognizing where we went wrong, but also about understanding why we went wrong and how we can right those wrongs moving forward. It's about turning hindsight into foresight, transforming past failures into future successes.

Implementing a Learning Culture: Encouraging Continuous Improvement

The idea of a "learning culture" is not a novel concept. It's been the subject of countless books, seminars, and executive retreats. Yet, despite the considerable buzz around the term, fostering a genuine learning culture remains a challenging task for many organizations.

At its heart, a learning culture is one where continuous improvement is not just appreciated but actively sought after. It's a culture where the collective ethos is governed by the pursuit of knowledge, skills, and the refinement of processes. It's about nurturing an environment where every experience - success or failure - becomes an opportunity for learning and growth.

In a learning culture, the responsibility of learning extends beyond the individual to the collective. Learning becomes a shared enterprise, a communal pursuit. This collective learning responsibility fosters a sense of solidarity and interconnectedness among team members, fortifying the bond that unites them.

Creating such a culture involves encouraging risk-taking and exploration. Employees should feel empowered to push boundaries, to venture into uncharted territories, and to make mistakes. Mistakes, after all, are not fatal flaws but steppingstones on the path to innovation and improvement.

Feedback, in a learning culture, is seen as a gift, not a threat. It is an invaluable source of learning, providing insights and perspectives that help individuals and teams improve. Leaders in a learning culture cultivate a feedback-rich environment, where constructive criticism is encouraged, and diverse perspectives are welcomed.

A learning culture weaves learning opportunities into the very fabric of everyday work. From on-the-job training and job rotation programs to project debriefs and team reflections, learning becomes an integral part of work, not a separate activity squeezed into busy schedules.

Moreover, in a learning culture, learning resources - be it training programs, online courses, mentoring opportunities, or learning tools - are made readily accessible. This ensures that everyone, regardless of their role or level in the organization, can learn, grow, and contribute.

By fostering a learning culture, organizations stand to gain manifold. It enhances their agility, allowing them to adapt to changes swiftly and effectively. It strengthens their resilience, equipping them to bounce back from setbacks and navigate challenges. It boosts their competitiveness, by driving innovation, enhancing skills, and improving performance.

In conclusion, implementing a learning culture is not just about promoting learning. It's about redefining how we perceive mistakes, how we give and receive feedback, and how we approach work. It's about encouraging continuous improvement, nurturing collective responsibility, and empowering employees. It's these elements that make a

learning culture more than just a buzzword, transforming it into a powerful catalyst for growth, change, and enduring success.

Turning Failures into Steppingstones: Using Setbacks to Propel Growth

The mere mention of the word "failure" often conjures up discomfort and apprehension. We, as a society, have been conditioned to view failure as an undesirable outcome, a stigma, something to be avoided at all costs. Yet, paradoxically, in the realm of business and innovation, failure is not just an inevitable occurrence, but also a powerful engine for growth.

Embracing this paradox requires a seismic shift in our perception of failure. Instead of viewing it as a sign of incompetence, it needs to be reframed as an integral part of the learning process, a steppingstone on the path to success. It's about acknowledging that each misstep carries within it valuable insights and lessons that can fuel our growth.

Creating an environment where failure is normalized is key to leveraging its potential. In many innovative companies, there is a saying: "Fail fast, fail often." This mantra reflects the understanding that the path to innovation is paved with trials, errors, and yes, failures. It is through a series of iterative experiments, and subsequent failures, that breakthrough ideas are forged. Thus, failure is not an end result, but a steppingstone in the innovation process.

Learning from failure, however, requires more than just acknowledging its existence. It requires the willingness to introspect, to delve into the heart of failure and extract the hidden lessons it contains. It requires the courage to admit mistakes, seek feedback, and make necessary changes. It's about using the experience of failure not as a deterrent, but as a springboard that propels us forward, wiser and more resilient.

In conclusion, turning failures into steppingstones involves embracing growth, reflecting on past missteps, fostering a learning culture, and reframing our perspective on failure. It's about harnessing the transformative power of failure to ignite a cycle of learning, innovation, and growth. It's about learning to navigate the fog of failure, and discovering the beacon of learning that lies within. As we leverage this beacon, we can steer our course towards a future of unbounded possibilities.

To quote Thomas Edison, an inventor whose persistence in the face of failure led to ground-breaking innovations, "I have not failed. I've just found 10,000 ways that won't work." As we learn to turn our failures into steppingstones, we too can inch closer to finding the ways that do work, driving us forward in our journey of continual growth and discovery.

CHAPTER 10

RISING FROM THE ASHES
TRANSFORMATIVE POWER OF FAILURE

Embracing Failure as a Launchpad for Success

In this chapter, we would delve into the transformative power of failure and explore how it can serve as a catalyst for growth and innovation. We would cover strategies for turning failures into steppingstones and discuss how a resilient mindset can help business leaders bounce back stronger from setbacks.

In business and in life, failure can often feel like the end of the road. It can shatter dreams, dent confidence, and incite doubt. Yet, there is another way to perceive failure - not as a pitfall, but as a launchpad for success. This chapter, "Rising from the Ashes: Embracing Failure as a Launchpad for Success," is dedicated to exploring this transformative power of failure and its potential to serve as a catalyst for growth and innovation.

In the unforgiving world of business, it's inevitable that we will face failures and setbacks. What's crucial is not the failure itself, but how we respond to it. Successful entrepreneurs and business leaders have one thing in common - resilience. They have an uncanny ability to weather storms, to stand up each time they fall, and to see failure not as a destination, but as a temporary detour on the road to success. This resilient mindset is a key element that helps business leaders bounce back stronger from setbacks.

But how does one cultivate such resilience? It begins with a shift in perspective. We need to view failure as an opportunity for learning and growth rather than as a symbol of defeat. When we make a mistake, it's essential to analyze what went wrong, what could have been done differently, and what lessons can be gleaned. These insights become the steppingstones that pave the way to future success.

Furthermore, failure is often a crucible for innovation. Many groundbreaking ideas and products were born out of failure. Take, for instance, the creation of the post-it notes. What started as a failed attempt to develop a super-strong adhesive resulted in a product that is now a staple in homes and offices around the world. When we start seeing failure as a breeding ground for innovation, we start finding opportunities where others only see dead ends.

Yet, embracing failure is not just about cultivating a resilient mindset or fostering innovation. It's also about creating a culture where failure is accepted and even celebrated. This means encouraging risk-taking, providing support in the face of failure, and celebrating the lessons learned rather than just the successes. It's about creating an environment where employees feel safe to fail, and as a result, dare to innovate.

In conclusion, failure can be a profound teacher, an unlikely ally, and a powerful launchpad for success. By redefining our relationship with failure, turning our failures into steppingstones, and fostering resilience, we can rise from the ashes of our setbacks and navigate our way to success. It's a challenging journey, but one that holds the promise of unprecedented growth, innovation, and success.

From Missteps to Mastery

In the tumultuous voyage of business, where the tides of uncertainty can steer a ship off course, failures are a given. They come unbidden, leaving trails of disappointment, doubt, and often, disillusionment. Yet, even in these disheartening moments, a beacon of hope exists - if we choose to see it. It's the promise of transformation, the potential for growth, and the pathway to mastery. This chapter, "Harnessing the Power of Failure: From Missteps to Mastery," aims to guide business leaders through this reframing process, turning the narrative of failure from a tale of regret into a saga of triumph.

The first step in harnessing the power of failure is learning from mistakes. Every failure, no matter how disheartening, carries a lesson. It's akin to a feedback mechanism, signaling that something in our approach needs to be altered. The key lies in honing our ability to decode these signals. This involves cultivating a mindset of curiosity and openness, asking probing questions, and conducting honest post-mortem analyses.

Yet, extracting lessons from failure is not a solo endeavor. It's a collective pursuit that involves soliciting feedback from team members, mentors, and even customers. It's about fostering a culture of transparency and psychological safety, where individuals feel safe to share their thoughts, observations, and insights. It's about learning to listen to the whispers of failure, for they can guide us on the path to success.

In the world of business, failure is often regarded as a detour to the journey of success. Yet, the stories of entrepreneurs who have failed and bounced back illustrate how failure, although tough to grapple with, can be the best teacher. This chapter, "The School of Hard Knocks: Building Knowledge from Business Failures," seeks to illuminate the role of failure as a catalyst for expanding our knowledge base, strengthening our business strategies, and cultivating wisdom.

Failure has a way of pushing us out of our comfort zones. When we encounter setbacks in business, we're forced to confront our limitations and challenge our assumptions. The strategies we had meticulously crafted and the plans we had confidently executed all come under scrutiny. This process, though uncomfortable, presents us with a golden opportunity to gain insights we may not have otherwise uncovered.

A prime example of this can be seen in the story of the tech giant, Apple. In the 1990s, the company launched the Apple Newton, a personal digital assistant designed for managing personal information. Despite the innovative concept, the product was a failure, mainly due to its high cost and technical issues. While this was a setback for Apple, it served as a valuable learning experience. The company used the insights gained from this failure to enhance their future products. The lessons learned from Newton's handwriting recognition technology failures later paved the way for the development of multi-touch interfaces, a key feature in their wildly successful iPhone and iPad.

The act of building knowledge from failure is a proactive process. It involves not only identifying the lessons from each setback but also deliberately integrating these insights into our future business strategies.

To accomplish this, creating a 'knowledge repository' can be instrumental. This repository can serve as a collection of lessons learned, meticulously documenting each failure and the insights gleaned from it. It serves as a reference guide for future decision-making, helping to ensure that past mistakes are not repeated.

The example of Henry Ford, the founder of Ford Motor Company, serves as an illustrative case. Ford's first venture, the Detroit Automobile Company, was a failure, mainly due to the high prices and low quality of its products. However, Ford used this failure as an opportunity to learn, reassessing his strategies, and incorporating the lessons into his next venture. His subsequent success in establishing Ford Motor Company and revolutionizing the automobile industry attests to the value of such an approach.

The Priceless Source of Wisdom

While the school of hard knocks can be harsh, it is undeniably a priceless source of wisdom. The challenges and setbacks we face in business failures have the potential to shape us, mold us, and provide us with a depth of understanding that textbook knowledge often falls short of.

The story of Arianna Huffington, co-founder of Huffington Post, illustrates this. Her second book was rejected by 36 publishers, a failure that could have dissuaded many. Yet, Huffington learned from this failure, gained resilience, and went on to launch one of the most successful online news outlets. The wisdom she garnered from her failure was instrumental in shaping her future success.

In conclusion, embracing failure as a tough yet enlightening teacher can transform the way we navigate our business journeys. By recognizing the insights failure unveils, mapping lessons into our strategies, and valuing the wisdom of our experiences, we can build a solid foundation of knowledge that propels us towards success. Remember, in the narrative of business, failure is not the antagonist but rather the wise mentor, guiding us towards our ultimate goals.

The Resilience-Forged Confidence

A popular myth is that failure equates to a lack of confidence, that each misstep in our business journey chips away at our self-belief. Yet, in "Boosting Confidence: Harnessing Failure as a Catalyst for Self-Assurance", this chapter contends that failure, paradoxically, can bolster our confidence. When we confront failures and navigate through the resulting challenges, we build resilience. We learn that we can survive the storms of adversity and emerge stronger. We gain confidence in our ability to solve problems, surmount obstacles, and turn around even the most challenging situations.

Resilience, the capacity to bounce back from setbacks, often serves as the crucible in which self-confidence is forged. The process of grappling with failure, of picking ourselves up and dusting ourselves off, lends us a newfound strength. It's akin to a sailor navigating choppy seas; each successfully navigated storm not only brings the sailor closer to their destination but also instills in them a deep-seated confidence in their sailing capabilities.

Let's consider the journey of Steve Jobs. After being ousted from Apple, the company he co-founded, Jobs could have wallowed in the failure. Instead, he chose to start NeXT, a computer platform development company. Although NeXT did not become the massive success Jobs had hoped for, it did not deter him. The lessons he learned and the resilience he developed during this period became the backbone of his later successes when he returned to Apple. The confidence Jobs derived from his ability to rebound from failure was instrumental in leading Apple to become the tech powerhouse it is today.

In order to foster this confidence-boosting aspect of failure, it's important to shift our perspective. We need to make a conscious effort to reframe failures as opportunities for learning and growth. This reframing process isn't always easy; it requires us to swim against the current of societal norms that often equate failure with incompetence.

What's key here is to celebrate not just the successes but also the courage to venture, the resilience to endure, and the wisdom to learn from failures. Commemorating the journey, the effort, the tenacity, and the grit that form the path to success can serve as a powerful confidence booster. It's about understanding that the road to success isn't a sprint but a marathon, and every step, whether forward or backward, contributes to the completion of the race.

The story of Thomas Edison illustrates this principle beautifully. Despite countless unsuccessful attempts at inventing the electric light bulb, Edison persevered. When asked about his failures, he confidently asserted, "I have not failed. I've just found 10,000 ways that won't work." This unwavering confidence in the face of failure, fueled by his commitment to the journey, ultimately led to his groundbreaking invention that forever changed the world.

In conclusion, viewing failure as a steppingstone rather than a stumbling block can profoundly transform our confidence. By consciously learning from our mistakes, actively building knowledge, and using these processes to boost our self-belief, we can harness the transformative power of failure. Our business journey becomes less about avoiding failure and more about evolving through it. This transformative journey is akin to the metamorphosis of a phoenix rising from the ashes of failure, resplendent in the confidence of its flight. After all, in the symphony of business, the music of success is composed not only of triumphant high notes but also the profound lessons hidden within the lower notes of failure. It's the harmony between these that orchestrates the melody of growth, innovation, and mastery.

CHAPTER 11

CEREBRAL VIEW
INTELLECTUALIZING BUSINESS DECISIONS

In the throbbing heart of today's business world, amidst the din of market fluctuations, competitive pressures, and technological advancements, a cerebral approach to decision-making stands as an oasis of calm and clarity. It represents a paradigm shift from reactive, emotional decision-making to a more deliberate, analytical, and strategic thought process. By adopting this approach, businesses can navigate the complexities of the business landscape with informed confidence, sidestepping the pitfalls of hasty decisions made in the heat of the moment.

As we dive into the digital era, data has emerged as a new kind of currency. But the true value of data doesn't lie in its mere accumulation; it lies in its analysis and application. Data-driven insights can provide a clear-eyed view of the business landscape, revealing patterns, trends, and opportunities that might otherwise go unnoticed. It can help businesses understand their customers better, fine-tune their operations, and make informed strategic decisions. In this section, we will explore various strategies for gathering, analyzing, and interpreting data, and how these insights can fuel effective decision-making.

It's a cognitive process that involves forming conclusions from a set of facts or premises, ensuring that our decisions are rooted in rational thinking rather than gut reactions. By developing strong logical reasoning skills, business leaders can improve their problem-solving abilities, make more confident decisions, and communicate their ideas more effectively. This section will delve into the intricacies of logical reasoning, providing practical techniques for honing these skills and applying them in a business context.

Success favors those who can look beyond the present and anticipate the future. Strategic foresight refers to the ability to identify emerging trends and prepare for future challenges and opportunities. It's about scanning the business environment, understanding larger socio-economic forces, and using this knowledge to steer the business ship in the right direction. This section will highlight the importance of strategic foresight in decision-making, outlining various tools and techniques for cultivating this crucial skill.

Data-Driven Insights and Decision Making

Competitive advantage in today's business world is as much about superior data literacy as it is about quality products or services. Every byte of data—whether it relates to market trends, customer behavior, or internal operations—can yield valuable insights that guide strategic decision-making, optimize operations, and enhance customer satisfaction.

Businesses can translate raw data into actionable insights, shedding light on different types of business data, techniques for data analysis, and ways to convert insights into strategy. We also explore the transformative potential of data visualization in making complex data comprehensible, engaging, and impactful.

Amazon and Google—two giants that have shaped the digital era—are prime examples of how data can be harnessed to drive growth and innovation. Amazon's personalized recommendations and Google's search algorithms are powered by the intelligent application of data. These case studies will provide readers with a practical understanding of how these companies have used data to refine their business models, understand their customers, and stay ahead of their competition.

However, as the saying goes, with great power comes great responsibility. In the context of data, this responsibility manifests itself in three main areas: data integrity, data security, and data privacy. Data integrity ensures that the data used for decision-making is accurate, consistent, and reliable. Data security protects sensitive data from breaches and cyber-attacks. Data privacy respects the rights of individuals and complies with regulations regarding the collection, storage, and use of personal data. This section underscores the importance of these ethical considerations, offering strategies for maintaining data integrity, ensuring data security, and safeguarding data privacy.

The Power of Logical Reasoning

Leaders often find themselves at the crossroads of decision-making, surrounded by a discord of information, emotions, and pressures. It is here that the power of logical reasoning stands as a beacon of clarity, guiding them through the fog of uncertainty towards sound decisions. Rooted in the principles of logic, it cuts through the noise and brings into focus the essence of the problem, the patterns in the chaos, and the way forward.

Embracing logical reasoning in business is about transforming the way we think, perceive, and decide. It's about stepping away from reactive emotional decision-making and moving towards a more objective, evidence-based approach. It involves replacing gut feelings and hunches with structured thought processes and reasoned arguments. This section provides an overview of the principles of logical reasoning and their role in effective decision-making.

Developing and strengthening logical reasoning skills is not an overnight process; it involves understanding and practicing various reasoning tools and techniques. These include problem decomposition—breaking down complex problems into smaller, manageable parts; cause-and-effect analysis—identifying the root cause of a problem and its impacts; and scenario planning—anticipating possible outcomes and planning for them.

Like any skill, logical reasoning improves with practice. This section offers strategies for embedding logical reasoning in everyday decision-making, from team meetings and project planning to strategy formulation and crisis management. It provides readers with practical exercises and techniques to hone their logical reasoning skills, transforming them from occasional tools to habitual thought patterns.

Harnessing Strategic Foresight

Strategic foresight is the binoculars that allows a business to look beyond its immediate environment and anticipate the coming curves in the road. As an integral part of modern business management, strategic foresight employs the power of projection and prediction, helping companies' future-proof their strategies and carve a pathway that navigates emerging challenges and seizes nascent opportunities.

In a world marked by flux and fierce competition, where markets pivot on the pinhead of innovation, foresight is no longer a luxury; it is a necessity. It means peering into the uncertainty of tomorrow and shaping today's decisions accordingly.

Showing how tools such as scenario planning, trend analysis, and predictive modeling can help businesses navigate the unpredictable currents of the business environment. It is about building robust, resilient strategies that stand firm amidst market volatility and emerge stronger from the crucible of change.

Scenario planning, a tool born from the military strategy rooms and adopted widely by businesses, is about envisioning multiple possible futures. It involves extrapolating current trends and envisaging different outcomes based on various influencing factors. By doing so, businesses can prepare for a multitude of potential realities, ensuring resilience and readiness, regardless of the turn of events.

Trend analysis, on the other hand, is about scrutinizing the trajectory of specific factors—be it consumer behavior, technology adoption, or socio-economic shifts—and analyzing their potential impact. It's akin to reading the currents of a river before setting sail; it provides businesses with the foresight to anticipate changes and adapt their strategies accordingly.

Then we have predictive modeling, a sophisticated data-driven tool that uses algorithms to predict future trends. Leveraging vast swathes of data and the power of artificial intelligence, predictive modeling can provide businesses with remarkably accurate insights into the future, from sales forecasts to consumer behavior predictions.

These strategic foresight tools, when wielded effectively, can give businesses the agility to pivot in response to anticipated market changes, the insight to innovate ahead of the curve, and the vision to seize opportunities before competitors even see them. In the chess game of business, strategic foresight can mean the difference between being a mere player and becoming the grandmaster.

Leveraging Technology: AI and Beyond

We are amid a technological renaissance where Artificial Intelligence (AI) is not just a futuristic concept, but a transformative force reshaping the contours of business. The vanguard of this revolution, AI, together with other technological advancements, is fundamentally changing how businesses operate and make decisions.

AI's transformative potential lies in its ability to convert vast amounts of raw data into actionable intelligence. Through machine learning algorithms, AI can analyze patterns in customer behavior, predict market trends, and even recommend strategic decisions, all with a speed and accuracy that outpaces human capacity. Business intelligence tools powered by AI can augment human decision-making, equipping businesses with insights that would otherwise be buried in the deluge of data.

Beyond AI, technologies like blockchain, Internet of Things (IoT), and augmented reality (AR) are also making waves in the business world. Blockchain's promise of a secure, decentralized ledger system can revolutionize industries from finance to supply chain management. The IoT, by connecting devices and systems, can provide real-time operational insights and optimize efficiency. AR can redefine customer experiences, offering immersive, interactive engagements that take personalization to a new level.

However, the deployment of these technologies is not without its challenges and ethical considerations. As we venture deeper into the realm of AI, issues of data privacy, algorithmic bias, and the digital divide become increasingly pertinent. This chapter will not just extol the virtues of technology but will also cast a critical eye on these challenges. We will discuss strategies for mitigating these risks, from ethical AI frameworks to robust data governance policies.

Case studies from industry pioneers who have successfully harnessed these technologies will offer readers a practical perspective. We will see how Amazon uses AI for predictive analytics, how IBM's Watson is revolutionizing healthcare, and how small businesses are tapping into the power of data analytics and AI.

It's about recognizing the transformative potential of AI and related technologies, navigating their challenges, and strategically employing them to gain a competitive edge. As we forge ahead into this exciting technological era, businesses that can ride the crest of this wave will not just survive but thrive.

CHAPTER 12

THE PHOENIX SOARS
SEIZING THE FUTURE WITH RENEWED VIGOR

As we turn the final page of our journey, it's time to reflect on the crucial lessons we've learned. We've navigated the rough seas of acknowledging our troubled situations, assessing the viability of our businesses, and making the difficult but necessary changes. Through these challenges, we've laid the groundwork for an exciting resurgence.

In reconnecting and rebuilding trust, we have reestablished our integrity and won back the faith of our customers and stakeholders. We have reassessed our capabilities, identified areas for growth, and begun the journey towards financial recovery. We have understood that our ability to innovate and adapt in times of distress is the key to our survival and success.

Our chapters on resilience in leadership, strategic partnerships, and learning from mistakes have equipped us with essential tools and knowledge to navigate the stormy seas of business. We have redefined failure, understanding it as a potent fuel that powers our journey towards success. We've learned the art of rising from the ashes, embracing our flaws, and harnessing them to build a stronger, more resilient business.

As we adopted a cerebral view of decision-making, we learned to replace emotion with logic and strategize with an eye towards the future. We came to understand the transformative power of technology, particularly AI, in driving business growth and success.

But this is not the end of our journey; rather, it's the beginning of a new chapter. A chapter where we apply our newfound wisdom, insights, and resilience to seize opportunities and overcome new challenges. Our mistakes and failures are now our steppingstones, our experiences now the foundation of our success story.

As we soar into the future like a phoenix reborn from the ashes, we carry with us the strength of our trials and tribulations, the wisdom of our past mistakes, and the courage of our unwavering resilience. We have not only survived but thrived in the face of adversity.

As we close this book, remember that the principles you've learned here are not just to be read but lived. Business, like life, is a constant journey of learning, adapting, and growing. The storm may have passed, but the lessons it has taught us will guide our path forward.

So, let's rise, let's soar, and let's seize the future with renewed vigor, for the world awaits us. And as we write our success story, let's not forget the trials that shaped us, the failures that strengthened us, and the journey that made us who we are.

To the future of endless possibilities, to the phoenix in each of us – let's soar!

ABOUT THE AUTHOR

Randy Eachus is a visionary entrepreneur who has spent over two decades carving out a name for himself in the world of marketing and advertising. Possessing an innate ability to think outside the box, Randy has harnessed his creativity to consistently develop innovative solutions that bring value to both businesses and individuals alike.

Born with an entrepreneurial spirit, Randy began his journey in the marketing and advertising industry at a young age. With over 20 years of experience under his belt, he has worked in various capacities, from strategic planning and account management to creative direction and campaign development. Throughout his career, Randy has collaborated with a diverse range of clients, helping them reach their target audience through engaging and memorable campaigns.

Randy's true passion, however, lies in helping others succeed. As a serial entrepreneur, he has established multiple businesses, each designed to empower individuals and organizations to achieve their goals. His ventures have spanned industries such as technology, education, and personal development, demonstrating his unique ability to identify emerging trends and capitalize on untapped market opportunities.